CIVIL WAR
EUFAULA

CIVIL WAR EUFAULA

★ MIKE BUNN ★

Charleston | London

THE
History
PRESS

Published by The History Press
Charleston, SC 29403
www.historypress.net

Copyright © 2013 by Mike Bunn
All rights reserved

Images courtesy of the author unless otherwise noted.

First published 2013

Manufactured in the United States

ISBN 978.1.62619.244.7

Library of Congress CIP data applied for.

In memory of my father, James Marshall Bunn, who taught me the virtue and value in hard work.

Contents

Preface

Early in the afternoon of Friday, January 11, 1861, a sudden commotion caused by the receipt of some rather remarkable news broke the calm of a peaceful, sunny winter day in the riverside trading town of Eufaula, Alabama. Within moments, a lone horseman emerged out of the escalating clamor of excited voices rising from the gathering crowd near the telegraph office downtown. Charged with carrying the momentous news that Alabama had just proclaimed itself an independent republic to the county seat of Clayton, he raced up Broad Street and ascended College Hill for his twenty-one-mile journey through the forest and fields connecting the two cities. The drumbeat that his animal's hooves thundered out as it galloped past stately homes drew the interest of residents on edge and aware that other Southern states had already seceded.

Anyone who had been paying attention to recent events had reason to suspect the gist of the message he carried, for he had made a similar ride only three weeks earlier when South Carolina became the first state to leave the Union. When the next state would make a similar move was discussed seemingly everywhere. At the very least, people knew from his rushed ride that he was on no ordinary errand. From the sidewalks of wagon-rutted dirt streets, within landscaped yards, seated in chairs on wide porches and from behind wavy hand-blown glass windowpanes, Eufaulians watched the rider hurriedly dash by and disappear over the crest of the hill. The moment was truly the last fleeting instant of calm before a terrible storm, and into the vacuum of normalcy it pierced would flood a deluge of anxiety that overwhelmed the hearts and minds of local citizens for the next four and a half years. Scarcely could those witnessing the scene imagine the degree of disruption soon to be experienced by the community.

This book attempts to tell in narrative fashion the story of that disruptive experience. It is an effort to relate on a personal level the saga of the Eufaula area during the Civil War. It is a story that, despite Eufaula's celebratory embrace of its heritage today, remains largely uninvestigated. I do not claim that what follows is *the* story of Eufaula's wartime years; there is simply too much we do not know and too much that can never truly be known to make such an assertion. Rather, I view this as more of a fleshing out of the bones of a story contained collectively in a number of other books and memoirs, letters and newspapers, official records and oral legends, each with different focuses and each recognized as important individually but never before woven together as a single tapestry.

To be blunt, we know incredibly little about Eufaula's Civil War years. Only a handful of the thousands living in the area at the time left written records of their experiences, extremely few copies of local newspapers survive and even the minutes of the city council from that period have been lost. Only the briefest of outlines of the city's wartime experience is currently interpreted in its various public history venues—house museums, the interpretive center, historic markers and parks. All we are left with from that dramatic era are scraps that we must mine and make logical inferences from if there is to be any real understanding of life in the city at the time. I am cognizant of the fact, though, that there will surely be other historians to investigate this topic in the future and unearth some things I did not during this project, enriching our knowledge with their findings.

I have written this story based simply on all the information I have found over the course of several years of research, a large portion of which is contained in the several histories of Barbour County and Eufaula and a portion of which exists only as oral interviews that inform these compelling local histories but can never be recovered. I have documented what I could and hopefully inferred only what I should in developing the rather piecemeal existing chronicle of Eufaula's Civil War years into a narrative tale that does justice to the incredible emotional and physical trials through which its citizens endured. Even if available records documenting Eufaula from 1861 to 1865 are not as voluminous as those from some other cities from the same period, there is nonetheless enough for us to understand the broad outlines of what life was like at the time. This story does not exist in a vacuum, after all; there is an abundant literature investigating the Civil War homefront experience in dozens of Southern communities, and while Eufaula's story is unique, it unquestionably has much in common with what is known about the wider region.

In composing this book, I have tried to focus on what seems to stand out as the most memorable shared experiences of area citizens, experiences that defined the era for those who lived through it. In other words, this is not the story of every aspect of the homefront experience, and no attempt is made at providing equality of space by topic or period; rather, it is the story of those aspects of life in the town during the war that resonate through the years as representative of a common passage through a tumultuous, watershed event. I need to mention at the outset that while my focus is obviously the city of Eufaula, I have chosen to include a range of sources from the broader immediate region as well. Eufaulians and those living near it during the era, just as those in and around the city today, share a regional connection that transcends municipal limits literally and figuratively.

Any good story needs a cast of characters, and a cast indeed can be found within these pages. Readers should know going in that extracts from the extraordinary diaries and correspondence of Barbour County residents Parthenia Hague, Elizabeth Rhodes, Victoria Clayton, John Horry Dent, S.H. (Hubert) and Anna Young Dent and young Mollie Hyatt form the core of the civilian perspective offered here. Their writings are among the most compelling and illuminating accounts of the war era to come from any Southern community, but they are also in a measure representative of a cross-section of the region's writing population—at least as representative

a sample of informed personal accounts from a town of Eufaula's size as one is likely to find. I use their observations to build a picture of an overall community experience rather than develop their individual personalities, but I have no doubt that readers will know and feel for them nonetheless as witnesses and players in a very real drama.

Eufaula diarist Elizabeth Rhodes. *Doug Winkleblack.*

Victoria Clayton around the time of the publication of her memoir in 1899. *Eufaula Athenaeum.*

At the outbreak of the Civil War, Parthenia Antoinette Vardaman, whose later married name was Hague, was working as a tutor to the children of the Garland family living near the community of Glennville. The community was at the time located in northern Barbour County (due to a later boundary change, it now lies in southern Russell County). In the 1880s, after her marriage, Hague published *A Blockaded Family: Life in Southern Alabama During the Civil War*, to critical acclaim. The book, praised by no less a figure than former Confederate president Jefferson Davis, recounts in detail many everyday events during the war while giving insight into the myriad ways locals attempted to adapt to wartime conditions. Just as crucially, it puts into words aspects of the emotional toll the conflict took on those in the Eufaula area.

Diarist Elizabeth Lewis Daniel Rhodes married local businessman Chauncey Rhodes in Eufaula in 1852 and lived there the rest of her life. She kept a diary at intervals from 1858 to 1900, providing insight on a variety of aspects of social life in the town. Her wartime entries, which compose the vast majority of the diary, are a colorful account of daily life in the city mixed with private thoughts. Her diary has, at long last, been published in full recently by the Eufaula Heritage Association as *The Diaries of Elizabeth Rhodes: Depicting Her Life and Times in the South from 1858 to 1900*.

Victoria Hunter Clayton, the wife of Confederate general and later University of Alabama president Henry D. Clayton, wrote the 1899 memoir *White and Black Under the Old Regime*, which recounts antebellum life in Alabama. At the time of the war, she lived on the family's plantation just outside the town of Clayton (there is no known connection between

Anna Young Dent and Stouten Hubert Dent. *Fendall Hall.*

her family and the name of the town), about twenty miles from Eufaula and the county seat of Barbour County. Her commentary on the war years especially illuminates aspects of slavery during the conflict and speaks to the anxiety associated with the arrival of Union troops in 1865.

New England native John Horry Dent moved to Barbour County from South Carolina in 1836, purchased some land just outside of Eufaula and began a long and successful career as a planter. Over time, his plantation, Good Hope, would become one of the most prosperous in the area. In his voluminous journals, extracts of which are published in *John Horry Dent: South Carolina Aristocrat on the Alabama Frontier*, are preserved accounts of the day-to-day operations of his plantation, his manner of dealing with slaves and his personal reflections on the Southern cause and the progress of the war.

Hubert Dent, a Maryland native who moved to Eufaula in the 1850s to practice law, enlisted in the "Eufaula Rifles," a local military unit, at the beginning the war. He eventually became an artillery officer in the Confederate army, leading "Dent's Battery" until the end of the war. He and his wife, Anna Young Dent, kept up a steady correspondence during the war. Much of it survives in the collections of the Auburn University Special Collections Library and the Alabama Department of Archives and History and is featured

Eufaula diarist Mollie Hyatt at age sixteen, immediately after the war. *Terry Honan.*

in *Fendall Hall: A True Story of Good Times and Bad Times on the Chattahoochee River.*

Mollie Hyatt was an eleven-year-old student boarding at Union Female College when the war broke out. The surviving portion of her surprisingly lucid diary chronicles a range of activities in Eufaula during the first year of the war.[1]

The individuals listed here are far from the only voices that can be heard in the pages to follow. The perspectives of fathers, mothers, sisters, brothers, husbands and wives are presented, as are those of political figures, businessmen, journalists, soldiers, housewives, students, visitors and even slaves where possible. The ultimate goal is the production of a mosaic of observations and a chronicling of milestone events that on some visceral level communicates a notion of what it was like to live through a cataclysmic and prolonged war that featured, at various times and in sundry ways, degrees of privation, worry, drama, celebration, humor and, on occasion, a deceptive sense of normality. It is the story of ordinary people in extraordinary times. It is my hope that it will both educate and entertain, for it is a labor of love and a small personal contribution to the rich legacy of a dynamic community that I am proud to say appreciates its past and has always encouraged me in my exploration of its history.

It is impossible to write a book without incurring many debts to those who helped at various points in the process. For assistance in the writing of this volume, I would like to thank especially former Historic Chattahoochee Commission executive director Doug Purcell for his insightful and thorough review of the manuscript, as well as his steadfast encouragement in my investigation of local history; Stephen Rowe of the Eufaula Athenaeum for his likewise close reading of my draft; and both Rowe and A.S. Williams III for generously making available rare pieces from the Athenaeum's rich collection for use as illustrations. I would also like to thank my friend and frequent collaborator Clay Williams for his careful review of this and so many other things I have written. The staff of the Alabama Department of Archives and History is deserving of recognition for the consistently courteous way they have dealt with my many inquiries. I sincerely appreciate Terry Honan making available to me the remarkable diary of his ancestor, Mollie Hyatt. Deborah Casey at Fendall Hall; Doug Winkleblack, current owner of Elizabeth Rhodes's home; and Rob Schaffeld all graciously loaned me images from their collections. The staff of the Eufaula-Barbour Chamber of Commerce generously allowed me to use their equipment to scan several loaned images. I appreciate the skill and patience of Marcolm Tatum, who created the custom map for the driving tour of historic sites and worked to adapt it for inclusion in this book A special thanks also goes to Scotty Kirkland at the Museum of Mobile for allowing me to borrow a phrase that perfectly describes Eufaula as well as his port city home, for both at times are indeed regarded as "encased in antebellum amber." Imitation is the sincerest form of flattery. Last but certainly not least, I would like to thank my wife, Tonya, and daughter, Zoey, for allowing me to work on this project when I could have or should have been doing something else with them. I appreciate their love and support more than they know.

Introduction

"The Business of Eufaula Is Large"

E ufaula is certainly one of the prettiest towns—I beg your pardon, it is already a city—through which it has been my good fortune to pass for many years" raved a correspondent for the *Macon Telegraph* after visiting the town in February 1861. Gushing at its prime location, the writer explained to his readers that the community was "pleasantly situated upon a high bluff, which renders it perfectly secure from the overflow of the Chattahoochee," and that a "well built lattice-work bridge" connected it with Georgia. He was struck by the "animated appearance" of the busy wharf, the epicenter of Eufaula's burgeoning economy, where he observed several steamboats that had docked whose crews were hurriedly loading cotton. All around gleamed signs of growth, prosperity and confidence in a bright future for the city of about two thousand in the Southern Confederacy. Many readers would have likely been surprised to learn that only a few decades prior, the bustling city had been a simple frontier settlement composed of a handful of makeshift buildings clustered along the bluff overlooking the river.[2]

Eufaula had risen quickly from its humble beginnings to become a regional economic, transportation and cultural hub for southeast Alabama and portions of southwest Georgia. Although the first American settlement near the ancient Creek town of Eufaula sprang up in the early 1820s, it was not until the next decade that the rough-and-tumble village began to take on the trappings of a real city. In 1834, Captain Seth Lore helped lay out the principal streets of Irwinton, as the community was then known (in honor of early benefactor William Irwin). The city quickly became a population center in the new county of Barbour, which had just been created in late 1832, as the rich agricultural lands of the region around the town lured an influx of American settlers into eastern Alabama. Following the defeat and forced removal of area Creek Indians after the bloody Second Creek War a few years later, a huge swath of eastern Alabama was officially opened to American settlement, and Eufaula's rise to prominence began in earnest.[3]

Gradually, the town expanded out westward from the river bluff throughout the next decade. Some of the older wooden buildings that originally overlooked the river were actually moved farther west on Broad Street, as that thoroughfare soon became the primary business center for the growing community. The stark contrast between the older section of town, featuring primarily weather-beaten wooden structures, and the newer developments, featuring several handsome brick buildings, must have been striking; visitors record that they were popularly known respectively as "Rotten Row" and "Brick Row."

Even with a relatively urbane business center at its heart, the city was decidedly not cosmopolitan in its early years, however. In the 1840s, street fights in Eufaula were not uncommon, and a major newspaper occupied a building that had once been a saloon and had bullet holes in the windows. Hogs roaming the streets and cows and pigs grazing in the city cemetery were still serious issues on the city council agenda, and vigilant respect for the Sabbath made the draying of goods from the wharf on Sundays illegal. Rapidly growing despite its ongoing concerns over the roamings of livestock, the community in 1843 officially reclaimed its original Creek name of Eufaula because, allegedly, residents thought that the name bespoke "something of an earlier age." According to legend, however, the change came at the behest of a prominent local businessman who had grown tired of having mail misdirected to the town of Irwinton, Georgia.[4]

Owing to a combination of geography, timing and hard work, Eufaula's economy boomed for the remainder of the antebellum period. By the eve of the Civil War, the city had laid claim to being the largest community in the sixth-most populous county in Alabama. Barbour County was home to more than thirty thousand residents in 1860. Over half were slaves. Sitting on the edge of the broad arc of the rich lands of the Black Belt, most of the county was ideally suited to agriculture. From the river to the county's western boundary, farms and plantations of all sizes dotted the landscape.

Due to its strategic location on the Chattahoochee River, Eufaula naturally became the trading center for this rich agricultural region. Rivers were the superhighways of the cotton trade in Alabama in 1860, and Eufaula emerged as a critical point of connection to regional and world markets via the Port of Apalachicola on the Gulf of Mexico. Innumerable bales of cotton, by far the chief export of the region, gathered from a radius of as many as fifty miles and sometimes more, were transported to Eufaula by wagon and oxcart and shipped down the Chattahoochee to ports as far away as New York and Liverpool. When the steamers returned, they often carried exquisite furniture and an array of fine goods in addition to copious amounts of dry goods, groceries and agricultural supplies for the growing markets in the Eufaula area. In just one steamboat shipment, for example, valued at more than $20,000, a Eufaula business partnership had delivered from New Orleans 1,200 bushels of corn, 250 barrels of flour, 150 casks of bacon, 120 barrels of pork and 100 barrels of whiskey. Summing the situation up concisely, a passing journalist reported that "the business of Eufaula is large."[5]

A scan of Eufaula newspapers from the era reveals a portion of the dynamic retail, service and industrial infrastructure in the city. Multiple grocery, dry goods and liquor stores offered a wide selection of goods, much of it imported "tariff free" directly from England. There was even a candy maker who proudly advertised that he sold "Southern Candy at Northern Prices." For other domestic needs, tailors, clothing shops, hat makers, furniture stores, cabinetmakers, jewelers and a bookstore competed for business. Eufaula even boasted a photographer's gallery for those who wished to "preserve their faces" through the cutting-edge technology of the ambrotype process.

Doctors, dentists and at least one obstetrician, as well as drugstores and the Eufaula Medical and Surgical Infirmary, catered to the medical needs of residents, including a partnership of four Eufaula doctors who operated an infirmary specifically for slaves. A metallic coffin supplier stood ready to provide a peaceful place of everlasting rest for those for whom these services were inadequate.

Two banks supplied financing for a range of capital needs, and insurance companies offered protection against their loss. There were wagon makers and a carriage dealer in town, and horse shoeing was readily available. A daily omnibus ran from downtown to the railroad across the river in Georgetown, Georgia. A marble works produced headstones, monuments and other stone products. The Eufaula Iron and Brass Foundry fashioned an impressive array of metal items to order including mills, gearing, grates, plows and weights, while nearby sawmills could convert the area's abundant timber into lumber to meet any construction need. And, of

Map of Alabama, 1859, with box showing Barbour County and Eufaula. *David Rumsey Map Collection.*

course, there were the Planter's and Chattahoochee Warehouses for the storage of cotton and auctioneers and commission merchants who offered to market the staple. Large stocks of goods were kept in hand at all times, "low river and acts of Providence excepted," advertised local businessman T.J. Cannon.[6]

It was cotton, "white gold," that greased the wheels of Eufaula's economy and brought about a remarkable concentration of wealth that catapulted it into urban sophistication. Evidence of the affluence of the city was not hard to find. Perhaps among the most visible manifestations were the many magnificent homes built in the city during this time on its broad, tree-lined boulevards. Wealthy planters, many of whom had extensive landholdings elsewhere in the county, built most of them even as they engaged in other business in town. The profits these enterprises produced facilitated a relatively luxuriant lifestyle that became the subject of much comment by visitors and residents. A local banker, for example, was remembered as having ridden in a silver-trimmed carriage, worn Irish linen and Scottish tweeds, drank Chinese tea and vacationed abroad every year. Many others, perhaps not as ostentatious but equally possessing of such means, more modestly wore the latest fashions, lived in the most lavishly decorated homes and subscribed to the most erudite journals the nation could offer.

The city's influence as a regional societal hotspot was not calculated in dollars and cents alone, though. In the latter part of the antebellum era, Eufaula rapidly became a dynamic cultural hub referred to by some as the "social metropolis of east Alabama." It was famed for dinner parties and dances on par with any in the South, boasted elite educational institutions for young men and women, hosted several fine churches and fraternal orders that formed its distinguished civic heart and served as venue for visits by heralded political figures, raucous rallies and festive barbecues that provided entertainment and forums for discussion of national events. Increasingly, the featured guests at these events were home-grown leaders as Eufaula began to assert itself on the statewide political scene.[7]

In 1861, Eufaula stood as a growing city in the heart of the lower South's plantation belt, experiencing some of the most dramatic growth in its short history. Over the course of the previous two decades, it had proven to be an attractive place for the ambitious to make their fortunes, and their mark on the world, through the lucrative opportunities presented by a developing city unencumbered with the imposing tradition of establishment. Its strategic location, enabling it to capitalize on global economic trends, had launched it into a brief era of prominence that was reflected on both balance sheets and ballots. Only two years earlier, a local newspaper had boasted of the city's recent coming of age, listing its numerous advantages and accomplishments and rhetorically asking readers, "Who will say Eufaula is not coming out?" On the brink of the outbreak of the nation's greatest trial, few could take issue with the statement. As the states of the Lower South set out to form a new nation, Eufaula had become a place of consequence and influence.[8]

Chapter 1

"Equality in the Union, or Independence Out of It"

The story of Eufaula's Civil War experience in many ways begins over a decade prior to the firing on Fort Sumter, with the efforts of prominent local residents to urge Alabama toward secession. Central to this effort was a group of men known as the "Eufaula Regency," which worked assiduously to convince fellow Southerners of the viability of secession. The group's coordinated actions dated back to as early as the 1840s. In 1847, for example, some of its members were among the twenty-one citizens of Eufaula who attached their names to a printed resolution arguing against the Wilmot Proviso, which would have prohibited slavery in the territory acquired by the United States as a result of the Mexican-American War. In 1850, some of its leading lights took part in the Nashville Convention, the first organized attempt of citizens of the Southern states to consider some form of united resistance to the North over the issue of slavery as debate over the Compromise of 1850 raged. While cooler heads ultimately prevailed and secession was postponed, the uproar that brought about the convention did have significant aftershocks that were felt across the South and even on the banks of Chattahoochee. Chief among these was the sudden rise of Southern Rights Associations.

Originating in South Carolina in 1848 to monitor perceived threats to the rights of slaveholders and the expansion of the institution of slavery, the Southern Rights Associations became powerful forces in Southern politics after 1850. William L. Yancey, a friend of several key Regency members and already widely recognized as a leading spokesman for

Southern interests on a national level, took the lead in urging the formation of associations throughout Alabama. Soon five centers of this "fire-eating" sentiment emerged as the loci of Alabama's nascent secessionist movement: Cahaba, Montgomery, Mobile, Jacksonville/Talladega and Eufaula. The Eufaula/Barbour County Association, in which the Regency played an important role, separated itself from its peers and established itself in the vanguard of the secession movement with its radical agenda. The association "embraced long-term agitation to convert the entire electorate to resistance" and desired to "launch a crusade to convince the citizenry of the justice of the southern rights cause." The group's members achieved remarkable success in giving their region of the state noteworthy political influence and "made them known throughout the South…as important in Alabama state politics as the Democratic Party political machine Tammany Hall was in New York."[9]

While the influence of the Regency is well documented in the historiography of the secession movement, stating precisely who comprised it is a difficult task. This is because the group operated a loose fraternity of Eufaula and Barbour County citizens with shared goals, not a formal organization with a charter, official positions or membership rolls. It would be from the rapidly swelling ranks of the city's lawyers— one historian of Eufaula has written that the young city "fairly bristled" with them—that many of its leading citizens of the era would come. As did men in similar positions elsewhere in the South at the time, many of these lawyers saw themselves as planters first and commonly held political aspirations above and beyond their legal careers. Primarily young self-made men who had carved out their position of influence through a combination of hard work and timely seizure of opportunities, they were seasoned by life in a frontier environment and well accustomed to speaking their mind. They were also as a group well educated and, as a result of their backgrounds and professional contacts, relatively sophisticated in their knowledge and understanding of national politics. Like so many ambitious and upwardly mobile young men of their generation in the South, they saw in the emerging sectional crisis both the institutional foundation of the society in which they lived and, just as importantly, their own future prosperity and opportunity for advancement gravely imperiled. As tensions began to mount over the issue of slavery, several of these lawyers banded together over shared interests in a determined effort to awaken their fellow Southerners to the import of events playing out on the national stage.[10]

The Eufaula Southern Rights Association,

WILL meet to-night at the Market House, to hear MAJOR BUFORD's Address, and appoint delegates to the State Convention. Jan. 21, 1851.

Notice of meeting of the Eufaula Southern Rights Association in the 1850s. *Alabama Department of Archives and History.*

Available evidence indicates that the Regency was led by the following: Alpheus Baker, Jefferson Buford, Edward C. Bullock, Lewis Lewellen Cato, Sterling G. Cato, Henry D. Clayton, John Cochran, James L. Pugh, Paul Tucker Sayre, Eli Sims Shorter, John Gill Shorter and Jeremiah N. Williams. From this small but influential group would come an impressive four members of the Alabama state secession convention, two secession commissioners, one member of the Provisional Confederate Congress, two members of the Confederate Congress, four Confederate army officers and a governor of the state of Alabama. Many other prominent citizens of Eufaula and the surrounding region, including newspaper publisher John Black; lawyer and later Confederate brigadier general Cullen A. Battle; lawyer, publisher and soldier Tennant Lomax; and lawyer, Confederate colonel and later governor of Alabama William C. Oates were also associated to varying degrees with the Regency. Several politicians and editors elsewhere in the state were also known to sympathize with the group, none more so than William L. Yancey. Yancey was not only one of the primary reasons for the group's existence by way of his support for the formation of Southern Rights Associations but also a constant ally of the Eufaula group and a personal friend of many of its members.[11]

The Regency formally announced its stance—and, informally, the extent of its local influence—on October 15, 1850, when the weekly *Eufaula Democrat* officially changed its name to the *Spirit of the South*. Featuring a masthead boldly proclaiming, "Equality in the Union, or Independence Out of It," editors Alpheus Baker and John Black (also proprietor) positioned the paper to become the foremost publication in the region to work in support of Southern interests, as well as the unofficial

Top: Eufaula Regency leader Alpheus Baker. *Eufaula Athenaeum.*

Bottom: Local political leader James L. Pugh. *Alabama Department of Archives and History.*

Eufaula Spirit of the South masthead. *Alabama Department of Archives and History.*

organ for the Regency. Later editors Edward C. Bullock and Paul T. Sayre would continue in the mission. The first few issues of the paper carried a succinct explanation of the *Spirit of the South*'s reason for being that clearly demonstrated its close connection with the local Southern Rights Association, as well as its bipartisan origins:

> *Whereas several members of the Eufaula Southern Rights Association of both political parties have conceived the idea of establishing in this place a paper called the "Spirit of the South," to be devoted exclusively to the maintenance of the doctrines advocated by the Southern Rights Party. Therefore, resolved, that this Association hereby recommends this paper to the confidence and patronage of all friends of the Southern cause.*[12]

The paper continually and forcefully agitated in favor of secession throughout the 1850s to a degree unrivaled in the state of Alabama and only rarely so in other Southern states. A leading forum for secessionist thought, it continued in publication until the latter part of the Civil War. It carried updates on the activities of other Southern Rights Associations in the region, regularly featured articles and editorials from around the South and nation discussing the growing sectional tension over the issue of slavery and closely followed debate over legislation that might affect the institution. The paper's editors even attempted to sway public opinion in favor of secession via rhyme. Editor John Black published several poems that set the viewpoint of the Regency and what it felt was at stake to verse:

> *Ye patriot whigs of old Barbour,*
> *Ye patriot democrats too,*
> *Your bright sunny south is in danger,*
> *She calls on her sons to be true.*

Our glorious loved constitution,
Abolitions' fell spirit would wield
To wrest from us rights 'neath its sanction
Of which it's the bulwark and shield.

Concession—we've made no concession
Borne insult, and outrage and wrong;
In forbearance, there'll soon be no virture
'Twill be found in secession before long.

The heritage won by our valor
Ye are robbed by a fanatic crew
And bright California never
Will yield her rich treasures to you.

When you gave up your rights in Missouri,
Acquiesced in the compromise line,
You thought abolition would slumber
You saw no ulterior design.

Her steps were at first slow and cautious
For patience she knew was her game;
But in the south's ear she now thunders
"To crush you's my end and my aim."

Already my girdle is round you
Already the rubicon's passed;
To your fate you must yield in submission,
I'll curb your proud spirit at last.

Your threats of secession are idle.
I treat them with scorn and disdain
You've threatened before—yet you've yielded,
You'll sink to submission again.

Ye men of the south, can ye longer
Brook language of insult and scorn;
Will you shout for the union hosanna
Till your rights and your honor is gone.

The union's a band of oppression.
'Tis oppression we ask you to meet;
Plant your feet on the old constitution
And strike, ere your ruin's complete.

Our fathers resisted oppression—
Fell bleeding for freedom and right,
Let their sons resist northern aggression
Have 36, 30, or fight.

Yes, sons of the south, to the rescue!
Your armour gird on and be firm
You can make the old captain surrender
And send Cochran to congress next term.

To the house, then send Shorter and Jason,
They're able, true southern rights men
In the senate place gallant Flewellen,
Leave Sanford at home to sooth Ben.

Then the patriots bosom shall gladden,
And full satisfaction be his;
We can read with a zest the "black numbers"
Of the shield as it was—as it is.[13]

When poetic invective proved insufficient to sway minds, the editors of the *Spirit of the South* lashed out at fellow Southern citizens who refused to join them in their crusade in a more personal way. As an example, when Benjamin Gardner, editor of the *Eufaula Southern Shield*, expressed his Unionist sentiments in the pages of his paper and attacked the *Spirit of the South* in sarcastic fashion, the Regency pounced. Under the tongue-in-cheek heading of "Elegant Extracts," the editors of the *Spirit of the South* published a series of statements allegedly made by Gardner that seemed to show his early support for the secession movement and portrayed him as a hypocrite. In later articles in their ongoing personal campaign against him, they labeled him unflatteringly as the "doughty champion of submission." Persistent, uncompromising and at times even personally vindictive, the Regency emerged as leading regional spokesmen for a cause in which it passionately believed. Concomitantly, it placed Eufaula in the vanguard of the movement it espoused through association, even as the majority of its fellow citizens had deep misgivings about its efforts.[14]

The Congressional campaign of 1851, in which the Regency was heavily involved, served to demonstrate just how reluctant the majority of the people of the region were about secession at the time. In that contest, the group supported John Cochran, a leading Regency affiliate and known secessionist, in his bid for a seat in the House of Representatives against Whig candidate James Abercrombie. Their friend and prominent fellow secessionist agitator William L. Yancey supported the cause and even spoke in favor of Cochran's candidacy at several public appearances during the campaign. Yet the contest became so bitter that a scheduled debate in Eufaula between the candidates had to be called off due to the tension it aroused. After Abercrombie ultimately won the election, Cochran's supporters sheepishly explained the loss by claiming that the prosperity of the times had simply blinded voters to the importance of the issues.[15]

The high point of the initial wave of secessionist sentiment that the Regency rode to prominence came after the presidential election of 1852. In that contest, the Southern Rights Party, a radical offshoot of the Democratic Party that the Regency and many like-minded citizens endorsed, nominated the aging George M. Troup for the nation's highest office at the convention in Montgomery after mainline party candidates Franklin Pierce and Winfield Scott failed to respond satisfactorily to queries posed by the group about their sensitivity to states' rights and sectional issues. The convention tapped John A. Quitman of Mississippi to run for vice president. Disaffected radicals from Cahaba, Montgomery and Eufaula, the very centers of secessionist activity in Alabama, dominated the Montgomery convention and pushed the nominations through. Barely registering enough support to merit mention in the election, Troup received votes in only Alabama and his home state of Georgia. He carried only two counties in Alabama, Lowndes and Barbour.[16]

The controversy that arose in the wake of the Kansas-Nebraska Act in 1854 brought about the most direct activism taken by any of the Regency's members and briefly placed the group in the national spotlight. A flashpoint for controversy during the sectional crisis of the 1850s, the act organized the Kansas and Nebraska Territories and opened them to settlement but left questions about slavery to be decided by the inhabitants of the region at a later date. As the more populous Kansas Territory rapidly moved toward statehood, it literally became one of the first battlegrounds on which the national debate over slavery would be played out. Prominent Regency member Jefferson Buford became one of the first in the nation to make an organized attempt to ensure that proslavery settlers moved to the Kansas Territory and provide the necessary votes to legalize slavery in the future state. Along with fellow Regency members Alpheus Baker, Edward C. Bullock, Henry D. Clayton and Lewis L. Cato, Buford openly denounced the efforts of such groups as the Massachusetts Immigrant Aid Society, which promoted the settlement of the territory by people opposed to slavery, and called on the Alabama legislature to fund an expedition to counter them. It is likely that these men and others in Eufaula may have been especially aware of the situation in the Kansas Territory through correspondence with Regency member Sterling G. Cato, who had recently moved to the area, but to date no correspondence between them has surfaced. Whatever his motivations, Buford ultimately decided to take matters into his own hands and launched his expedition from Eufaula on March 31, 1856.[17]

The citizens of Westport, Kansas Territory, welcomed Buford and his men when they arrived in May 1856, but the goodwill proved to be short-lived. Armed as territorial militia by the local government, Buford's men soon became involved in scattered fighting with free state settlers in the Lawrence area and were eventually accused of wanton destruction of private property. The group's organization broke down in the chaos of "Bleeding Kansas," and several men chose to simply quit and return home—or, in some cases, actually enlist with United States troops—rather than continue with their mission. Finding little additional financial support available and discovering that his expedition had virtually disbanded, Buford was forced to cut his losses, abandon his effort and make his way back to Alabama.[18]

Nonetheless, as tensions steadily mounted in the latter part of the 1850s, the Regency could claim to be winning more and more converts to its mode of thinking. Increasingly divisive political discourse had brought about a bitter brand of sectionalism in which the actions of one side were invariably viewed with suspicion by the other. Across the South, a growing number of citizens came to understand the debate over slavery as a zero-sum game—what the Regency had been shouting for all to hear for a decade. By 1858, even the *Eufaula Express*, a newspaper that competed with the *Spirit of the South* for readership, had placed on its banner the motto "A Southern Confederacy—The Sooner the Better" as a growing sense of Southern nationalism began to manifest itself on every level of public discourse in the town. Not to be outdone, the *Banner*, published in nearby Clayton, by early 1860 had changed its masthead to an ultimatum, "Separate Nationalities for Antagonistic Peoples."

Top: Outspoken local secessionist Jefferson Buford. *Alabama Department of Archives and History.*

Bottom: Regency leader and Confederate officer Henry D. Clayton as he prepared to embark for Kansas Territory in the 1850s to participate in the attempt to have Kansas enter the Union as a slave state. *Eufaula Athenaeum.*

Regional pride and increasingly vitriolic exchanges between respectively partisan Southern and Northern leaders helped finally swing into motion a range of activities that fit right into the longstanding plans of the Regency. This became especially apparent as it became clear that Abraham Lincoln—perceived as a sectional candidate hostile to the rights of Southern slaveholders—might actually win election to the nation's highest office. At last, a groundswell of public support for an independent Southern nation spilled out into open threats of disunion by vocal minorities throughout the South. On the eve of the fateful presidential election of 1860, which ultimately brought Lincoln into office, a group of Regency members, anticipating that result, wrote to Alabama governor A.B. Moore suggesting that he schedule a convention to discuss secession immediately after the election and calmly awaited the result of the contest.[19]

Chapter 2

"There Was Never Such a Time in Eufaula Before"

News of the election of Lincoln sent a shockwave through Eufaula and finally galvanized a majority of the community in favor of secession. Public reaction revealing the emergence of (and in some cases, the reemergence of) widespread prosecession sentiment was immediately evidenced. As soon as the results of the election became official, several people gathered to hastily erect a symbolic gallows at the intersection of Broad and Eufaula Streets (allegedly where the Confederate Monument now stands), where the president-elect was hung and burned in effigy. Elsewhere, the local militia units Eufaula Rifles and Pioneer Guards assembled and began to drill in preparation for what seemed to be an inevitable conflict. When the Guards met to elect officers, the men also took the opportunity to go a step further and unanimously resolved, in a display of Southern nationalistic pride, that the unit's uniforms should be made exclusively of goods produced in the South. Within days of the election, a proclamation signed by forty-eight prominent Barbour County residents calling for unity in the time of crisis circulated:

To the People of Barbour County

The abolitionists have triumphed. Shall we submit? Will Alabamians permit abolitionists to rule them? Shall we yield like slaves or resist like freemen? The great question we must now decide.

> *The country demands counsel of her citizens and we call upon the people of Barbour County to assemble at Clayton, November the nineteenth to deliberate and act. Come Southern men of all parties. Shut up the doors of your business houses and leave your plows in the furrows and let us take counsel together. The South demands union of her sons. Let us bury the hatchet of past divisions and come together at the appointed hour and like brothers prepare for safety and resistance.*

At the gathering on November 19, those assembled called for Alabama's immediate secession amid a festive rally featuring speeches and demonstrations by militia units.[20]

Locally and abroad, Eufaula's political leaders swung into action in short order to take the lead in making it clear to all who would listen what they believed the election signified. In early December, Judge John Gill Shorter, known to refer to the existence of a "Yankee race" inimical to the Southern way of life, addressed a large crowd in Clayton and claimed that the venerable United States Constitution had been "trampled beneath the feet of the invading foe," which operated under "the black banner of abolition." Shorter claimed that the election portended nothing less than Northern "dictation and control" of the South. With florid invective, he declared that, had he the power, he "would thunder amid the granite hills of New England, and echo along the rivers and lakes of the North, and reecho back from the icy cliffs of the Rocky Mountains, the glorious response, Alabama never surrenders!" In closing, he offered pointedly that "the government which our fathers made for us and our posterity has been overthrown... never to return."[21]

Simultaneously, Congressman James L. Pugh, in the nation's capital, offered the same sentiments to an even larger audience. In a public letter to his constituents, he cited the "destruction of the Federal Government, by the election of Lincoln" as his rationale for energetically and immediately promoting the cause of secession. "I believe much good can be done and evil prevented by the presence of Southern members," confided Pugh to those back home, asserting that he would do all in his power "to secure the speedy deliverance of the Southern people from the thralldom of an Abolition government." In language that vied with Shorter for creative use of hyperbole, he observed that Alabama, by its negative response to Lincoln's victory, had already put forth no less than a "second declaration of independence." He hoped that historians would "record it, and our posterity celebrate it, as the cause that secured to them the blessings of a Southern Confederacy."[22]

In private correspondence and journals, many Eufaula area residents wrote in similar veins of defiance and commitment to an as-yet-formed Southern nation. Elizabeth Rhodes wrote in her diary that "as has been feared Lincoln the Republican candidate is elected. Every true Southerner is for resistance." She expressed the feelings of many caught up in the moment by declaring that "we feel that we can never submit to the reign of so great an enemy to our institutions." Another local resident seconded her stance, writing in equally definitive terms that "if the South does submit, then I shall either emigrate or shut up about Southern Rights and Southern equality." Another lady wrote to a friend around the same time casting forward on the prospects of a Southern nation, melodramatically noting, "The only thing that gives me real pride is, that my child may be born in a Southern Republic and not in the detestable Union." The day after news of Lincoln's victory became official, Hubert Dent wrote straightforwardly to his wife that he felt like "the South now expects every man to do his duty." Whether there might be a diplomatic resolution to the impasse or an ensuing military conflict was all the talk on the streets of Eufaula. From the city's highest officeholders down to its most private of citizens, however, there was a shared understanding that a fateful moment of decision, years in the making, had arrived.[23]

Tension marked the weeks between the presidential election and the secession of South Carolina. When the Palmetto State became the first Southern state to leave the Union on December 20, 1860, a torrent of emotional release swept across the South like a tidal wave. Eufaula and Barbour County were among the first to feel its surge. The news appears to have first arrived in the county via telegram in Eufaula just minutes after the final vote was recorded. The electric shock of the announcement no doubt caused the crowd that had already gathered around the office, waiting for news of South Carolina's decision, to go into a frenzy and brought virtually all activity in Eufaula to a halt.

Within minutes, townspeople began gathering to nervously discuss what it all meant. Before the news even became general in Eufaula, a messenger was dispatched on the twenty-one-mile journey to Clayton to inform the county seat of what had transpired. According to local oral tradition, a black man named Lewis Jones, who presumably had performed the duty previously, was entrusted with the mission. Wearing a broad-brimmed hat, he made a straight line for Clayton as fast has his animal could carry him. When a citizen along the way tried to hail him to discern his hurry, likely realizing that he carried word of important news, he allegedly shouted as he passed that he could not stop because "South Carolina done seed sumthun."

No doubt the wording of his message derived from a corruption of what he was told to repeat upon arriving in Clayton—that South Carolina had seceded—pronounced at the time as "see-seeded." The horse Jones rode became known in Eufaula as the "telegraph horse."[24]

"There was never such a time in Eufaula before," recorded Elizabeth Rhodes in her diary the day of South Carolina's secession. The militia companies' cannons, standing in surprising but perhaps revealing readiness, were soon booming in celebration and flags "floating in the breeze in all directions." That night, a "great illumination" took place, as throughout the town bonfires were set ablaze in the streets, and military companies marched in a torchlight procession. "Twas the most gloriously magnificent sight I can behold. Almost every house appeared as if studded with diamonds in a glorious sunlight," recorded Rhodes. Fireworks sparkled in the night sky, and the local militias were out in force putting on demonstrations and stopping at the homes of prominent citizens, including Mayor William Thornton's, calling for speeches. Parties sprang up at many homes. According to legend, Lewis L. Cato threw one at his home in Eufaula that was attended by none other than William L. Yancey.[25]

Even had they held any reservations about the actions of the South Carolina legislature, citizens could scarcely have voiced them in such an environment. After receiving refreshments at several of the homes, the militiamen proceeded to the heart of downtown, where much of the city had gathered to present them with "an elegant repast." There the assembled crowd heard more patriotic orations and sang "two soul stirring songs composed for the occasion" as the festivities carried on late into the night. The celebration continued throughout the holiday season, as yuletide "secession parties" were thrown in both public spaces and private Eufaula homes. Early in the new year, one Eufaula resident proudly displayed a fifteen-star flag from the cupola of her home on College Hill, symbolizing a perhaps ambitious notion of the membership of the forthcoming Southern nation. The Eufaula Rifles saluted it with a fifteen-round artillery salute. Not to be outdone, the Pioneer Guards carried its own gun up the hill and did the same.[26]

After the initial jubilation, residents began to reflect soberly on coming events. In December 1860, Elizabeth Rhodes wistfully recorded that the "remarkably eventful year of 1860" soon would be over. With prescience, she observed on New Years Eve that "many events have occurred which will be handed down to posterity as important items of a nation's history... There are dark clouds overspreading our National Horizon and we cannot yet know whether the fringes of prosperity will dispel them and the bright rays of peace and happiness once more beams upon us, or whether they will grow darker and denser until proved out in wars and bloodshed on our once prosperous and happy nation. Time alone can unfold these things. We can only wait and pray God to overrule all things for His glory and the good of mankind."

On New Years Day 1861, John Horry Dent took stock of the turmoil engulfing the nation: "The year opens full of troubles to these once United States. Discord reigns supreme. The house is divided, and a breakup is inevitable. How it will terminate God alone can foresee. The South secedes from the Union, owing to northern aggression, and determinations to interfere with our Negro property, a southern confederacy is our only honorable and safe course."[27]

There were a great many in the Eufaula area who shared Dent's reasoning before the die had been cast in Columbia, South Carolina, and even more who came to applaud it after the fact. Some were blunt in their assessment of the options. Victoria Clayton reasoned that the South was forced into leaving the Union on practical grounds:

> *We of the South felt that we had become slave-holders under our common government with its most sacred sanction, and, being an agricultural people, our property consisted mostly of slaves. Our Northern brethren were a manufacturing people, their property consisting of factories of various kinds, likewise with the most sacred sanction of our common government. We of the South looked to this, our common government for the protection of our property, and felt that we did not receive this protection…There no longer is any room for hope. We must fight.*

In defiance of what he viewed as the North's adherence to rule by a "raw majority," in Congressman Pugh's last speech to the House in January 1861, he advanced a view of the construction of the Constitution that maintained that federal power rested with "the concurrent action of the people of each State by virtue of their sovereignty and independence." He noted matter-of-factly, "There is no value in the checking power of minorities, when selfishness, bad faith, and reckless construction break over constitutional limitations and guarantees," and called for "the formation of another union of States, homogeneous in population, institutions, interests, and pursuits" as the only logical course of action. "Such a confederacy would be imperishable," he believed. In the fervor of secessionist spirit in Eufaula in the first days of 1861, there were few who would disagree, at least publicly.[28]

Privately, though, even the most ardent Southern nationalists in the Bluff City were sometimes prone to expressing misgivings about where all the bombast might lead. In part, this had to do with the simple fact that the Union of which they had been a part their whole lives had been torn asunder so quickly with nothing concrete to take its place and near-certain strife ahead. One Eufaula resident wrote to a niece with resignation that "I regret very much that the Union is dissolved yet I had much rather for it to be so than be under the jurisdiction of such a [illegible] enemy to the South as that staunch abolitionist Lincoln is."

Overwhelmingly, though, any uneasiness about the future had more to do with the seemingly certain military conflict than ties to the Union. Anyone with any knowledge of current events in January 1861 knew that the possibility of war loomed in the not-so-distant future. Elizabeth Rhodes jotted down that although everyone seemed to be "excited on subject of disunion," she still hoped that "a merciful over-ruling Providence may so order every movement that all things may be settled without blood-shed." Quickly coming to the realization that war seemed certain, she noted resignedly a short time later that "perhaps some of the best blood of Southern sons will be spilt in defending what they believe to be their right." While she "rejoiced to know that we are no longer a part of the Union which would make us slaves…the signs of the times indicate much trouble." Parthenia Hague conveyed even more forthrightly that at that moment "we were by no means elated at the thought that our own noble commonwealth had seceded from the sisterhood of states. Feelings of sadness…overcame us." A short time later, John Horry Dent would confide somewhat ruefully in his diary that "thus has ended the Works of our Patriotic fathers of 1776."[29]

Alabama, given its role in fomenting the ideology of disunion, would naturally be at the forefront of the rush toward Southern independence in the wake of the election of Lincoln. Indeed, as one scholar of the period has noted, given the outspoken extremists operating within the state's political system, "if South Carolina had a sister state in secession, it was Alabama." Even before South Carolina's convention had cast its fateful vote in December 1860, Governor Andrew B. Moore had publicly declared that he could see no other course than secession for the state. The legislature in 1859, after all, had seen fit to authorize him to call a referendum for the election of delegates to a convention to discuss that very move should a Republican win the presidency. Moore called for that vote to take place on December 24, 1860, and its delegates met in Montgomery on January 7, 1861. The terribly divided mind of the state, and by extension the relative power of the growing disunionist faction within it, is revealed by how closely contested the vote for delegates became. Only one county in the southern half of the state chose to be represented by a man openly favoring continued cooperation with the federal government (Conecuh), while only one county in northern Alabama voted for men who could be counted on to cast a ballot in favor of secession (Calhoun). As debates began, though, secessionists were in a slim but clear majority, and the convention's ultimate direction seemed certain.[30]

Eufaula and Barbour County were, of course, well represented by firebrands in the convention. Among the group of men that ultimately led the state out of the Union were two of the old Regency's most recognized spokesmen, Alpheus Baker and John Cochran. Cochran became among the first to advocate for preparedness for the looming military contest, introducing a resolution in the legislature calling for the governor to seize preemptively federal arsenals and forts within Alabama's boundaries so that the state could utilize them in its defense. Also prominent in deliberations were other Regency members serving as appointed commissioners who functioned as advisors and correspondents with the governments of fellow Southern states to ensure coordinated action. These included John Gill Shorter, who was sent to Georgia, and Edward C. Bullock, who was sent to Florida.[31]

Both commissioners' later reports evidenced general enthusiasm for coordinated action among state leaders. Shorter opened his communication with officials in his native state with a flourish of hyperbole: "Alabama sends greetings to her mother—glorious old Georgia, the Empire State of the South—one of the immortal thirteen which suffered, and endured, and triumphed in the Revolution of 1776." Then he moved on to the task at hand. Drawing on the two states' commonalities and a decade in advancing the Southern cause in public discourse, he said that "Alabama invokes her [Georgia's] counsel and advice, her encouragement and cooperation. Having similar institutions, kindred sympathies, and honor alike imperiled, will not Georgia unite with Alabama and sister States in throwing off the insolent despotism of the North, and in the establishment of a Southern Confederacy, a government of homogenous people, which shall endure through all coming time the proudest and grandest monument on the face of the earth?"

In his summary report filed after the secession of Florida, just a day prior to Alabama's, Bullock stated happily, if somewhat grandiosely, that he had been greeted by Florida's governor, secession convention and the general citizenry of the state with "warmth and cordiality." He took heart at observing "the most gratifying proof that the strong ties of a common cause, a common danger and a common destiny, were deeply felt and appreciated, and the best reasons for hoping that the two States, divided by but a single day in the exodus from a Union of 'irrepressible conflict,' will soon be closely joined in that new Union of brotherly love, in which a homogenous people, taking their destiny into their own hands, shall exhibit to the world the noblest phase of Free Government, and the highest development of true civilization."[32]

The fateful vote of Alabama's secession convention occurred at about 2:30 p.m. in the afternoon on Friday, January 11, 1861. By a vote of sixty-one to thirty-nine, the Republic of Alabama was proclaimed. Immediately, the telegraph wires connecting Montgomery with the rest of the state and the South were abuzz with activity. A sixty-round cannonade salute greeted the news when it arrived in Eufaula. Church bells began ringing as the militia companies once again assembled in similar fashion to what had occurred just three weeks before. Once again, Lewis Jones rode his famous horse to Clayton to relay the message. Again there were fireworks, parades, bonfires and speeches heralding the occasion, as "shoutings filled the air" and "much of the city was illuminated." Young Mollie Hyatt at Union Female College recorded in her diary that "the cannon shot a hundred times this evening because Alabama seceded." She noted innocently that all the noise made her "very afraid."

Prominent local citizens turned out again to give public addresses praising the decision and celebrating the salient moment. Regency member Jeremiah N. Williams was one of several to address a raucous crowd in Clayton at a party that lasted into the early hours of the morning. The festive atmosphere continued throughout January and well into February 1861, with periodic concerts and speeches as other Southern states joined Alabama in leaving the Union. By the beginning of February, a brotherhood of seven states had seceded. Each sent delegates to Montgomery to form a new government. The formation of a Southern Confederacy and who its leaders might be instantly became the dominant topic of conversation on the streets, in the trading houses and in the parlors of homes throughout Eufaula.[33]

Delegates from the seceded states met in Alabama's crowded capital city during February and March 1861 to hammer out the document that would create and lay the foundation of government for the new nation. Again, a leading light from the Regency sat in attendance and figured prominently in the proceedings. John Gill Shorter served throughout that

Rendering of the Alabama Secession Convention flag. *Rick Wyatt, CRW Flags Inc.*

organizational session, with duties ranging from being a part of the special committee assigned to find offices for the new nation's executive department to serving on the welcoming committee for President Jefferson Davis (who had been elected as the new nation's chief executive), as well as serving as a member of committee appointed to notify Alexander Stephens that he had been elected provisional vice president. Shorter also helped frame the Confederate constitution and sat on two standing committees—Executive Department and Engrossments. As chairman for the Engrossments Committee, Shorter presented a specially prepared copy of the provisional Confederate constitution for signatures of delegates on the fateful day of February 18. With visions of the Founding Fathers in 1776, many signed with their own pens and kept them as mementos. Many certainly anticipated that paintings, similar to those of the Founding Fathers, would be made of them and likewise celebrated by future generations.[34]

Later in the year, Shorter would make the biggest splash on the political scene by Eufaulians and all who had embraced the cause of secession in Barbour County when in August he won election as governor of the state of Alabama. A few Regency members reputedly began his campaign, but

Wartime governor of Alabama John Gill Shorter. *Alabama Department of Archives and History.*

his role in establishing the provisional Confederate government and as a secession commissioner certainly helped make his name a recognizable one throughout the state. As a consequence of his posts in the convention and his longstanding position within the Regency, he also had enjoyed much crucial newspaper support throughout the state. His inauguration took place at noon on December 2, 1861, with Shorter becoming the first state governor elected under the Confederate flag.

In what must have certainly seemed like a triumphant vindication of more than a decade of effort to shape public opinion, one of the most respected Regency members had taken office as the state's chief executive. In a speech delivered to the legislature soon after the election, he concisely offered his thoughts regarding where the state and its compatriots had come from and where they were going. "We may well congratulate ourselves and return thanks that a timely action on our part has saved our liberties, preserved our independence, and given us, it is hoped, a perpetual separation from such a government." In predictably defiant rhetoric, he closed by demonstrating that he was committed to continuing to fight for Southern rights, offering a vision of the future for the Southern nation separate from the United States that was part hope and part ultimatum. "May we in all coming time stand separate from it, as if a wall of fire intervened." He could not have anticipated how literal that "wall of fire" would become, as the nation would soon become embroiled in a bitter and consuming civil war that would claim the lives of hundreds of thousands. He and other men of his ilk had long predicted a war, however, and they earnestly believed that they would win it.[35]

Chapter 3
"We Have Seen a Good Deal of It in Several Papers"

At precisely 4:30 a.m. on Friday, April 12, 1861, Captain George S. James ordered Lieutenant Henry S. Farley to pull the lanyard and fire a mortar from Confederate-held Fort Johnson to lob a shell at Union-occupied Fort Sumter in Charleston Harbor. The long, arcing solitary shot signaled the beginning of a general bombardment that would continue for the ensuing thirty-four hours. Long before the cannonade fell silent, the echoes of that round were reverberating across the nation. The long-prophesied civil war had begun, and the contest quickly found its way into the homes and hearts of the residents of Eufaula. What the fighting portended and who might be caught up in its grisly casualty count were issues of vital importance that consumed the city for more than four years.[36]

Concern with military matters in Eufaula actually began months before that first shot in Charleston Harbor. Local militia companies, realizing that they might soon be called on and desiring to seize the rare chance for battlefield glory, were preparing for deployment to whatever post they might be assigned to at the time of secession. The preparation of these companies featured somewhat regular celebratory and ostentatious drilling in the streets, formal reviews and a variety of public events. Mollie Hyatt recorded witnessing special militia displays twice in January 1861 alone, including one at which a company literally marched right into a church she was attending. Elaborate speeches preceded the presentation of homemade flags, and cannons fired periodically as military units paraded past adoring crowds. Stores closed early at times so that owners and employees could drill in newly organized units. To the unending delight of bystanders, the Eufaula Pioneers wheeled out their cannon, "Little Fire-eater," and fired the occasional salvo. A general, pervasive excitement in anticipation of a short but glorious war filled the air for weeks in the city. A visiting newspaper reporter in February 1861 noted the overt display of eagerness of the local troops and seemed to be impressed, asserting that "if there is any fighting to be done," the Alabama boys "will be found in the van."[37]

The desire of local young men to serve at first outstripped the capacity to put them into service, however, as many anxious volunteers were mustered into the ranks and drilled despite having no arms to bear. Local citizens such as Mrs. Roxanna Bethune Wellborn and Mrs. B.F. Treadwell did what they could to remedy the situation through their own resources and effort. Wellborn traveled to meet personally with President Davis and Confederate secretary of war LeRoy Pope Walker to make a special request for equipment. She must have been persuasive if accounts are accurate, because not only did they grant the request, but apparently she also convinced the new nation's leaders to allow her to bring the needed weapons and supplies back with her on the return journey rather than wait to have them shipped. Treadwell reputedly paid for the uniforms of Eufaula Rifles.

Private funding for military preparedness held true in the wider region, as well. William C. Oates, a young lawyer who had trained in Eufaula under some of the leading lights of the Regency before setting up an office in Henry County, visited the city on his way north as the war began and literally ran up the steps of the Eastern National Bank to cash a check for $2,000 given to him by Abbeville's citizens to buy supplies for the men of the company he had raised, the Henry Pioneers. In fact, expressions of support of the Southern cause, both financial and symbolic, became ubiquitous in Eufaula early in the war. The wearing of cockades as a symbol of unity became so common that local ladies began a virtual cottage industry of their production in town, and copies of Alabama's ordinance of secession could be purchased at J.A. Hunter's bookstore to be "preserved as an heirloom" proclaiming "Alabama Free, Now and Forever!"[38]

Filled with a fierce patriotism that derived from sheer love of home and the life they knew, but undergirded by vague and self-serving notions of constitutional principles, many of the young men rushing to volunteer simply hoped for a chance to win military laurels before the fighting concluded. Most thought that the war would be a quick one, and those who wanted to fight desired to be the first sent to the front lest they miss out on being a part of the event of their lifetimes. While we have no record of the thoughts of the overwhelming majority of local soldiers, men such as Hubert Dent likely spoke for many when he confided in a letter his personal conviction regarding the necessity of military service in support of the Southern cause. With stark simplicity set against a backdrop of what he understood as apocalyptic circumstances, he observed that "I feel like the South now expects every man to do his duty…It is absolute submission to Black Republican Rule or absolute resistance." The call to serve moved men from virtually all walks of life in the community. Even Bowman Seals, a free black man living in Barbour County, wrote to President Jefferson Davis offering his services as a soldier. Even if Seals had ulterior motives in his request, given his precarious status in a slaveholding society that inherently doubted his loyalties, his situation nonetheless surely paralleled the angles of many who rushed to the colors in the Eufaula region; convictions aside, the war might be a ticket to adventure and status if nothing else.[39]

Events moved so quickly that even close relatives sometimes first heard about enlistments of family members secondhand or barely had time to say goodbyes before loved ones marched off to the front. Parthenia Hague, then working as a tutor for a local family on a plantation north of town, remembered that she was on the way to her school one morning when she met a slave sent to retrieve the mail who handed her a note informing her that her brothers in Harris County, Georgia, were preparing to embark for Virginia, the epicenter of the front lines of the war at the time. She hastily journeyed to her home just in time to see them off, afterward providing a solemn and gripping account of her emotional return that surely bespoke the emotions so many in her situation were feeling:

> As I looked from the window of the speeding train to the dark green gloom of the almost unbroken forest, the low wail of the wind in the tops of the pines, the lowering dark clouds dimly outlined through the shaded vista, pressed down my heart as with a great sorrow; the far way mutterings of thunder, the low moan of the wind as it rocked to and fro the tops of the pines, came to me as the Banshee's lonely wail. All seemed to presage some dire affliction. Could it be that my father's household had joined together for the last time in their earthly home? Poe's ghastly, grim, and ancient raven seemed to speak the "Nevermore"; and, alas! Nevermore did we children of that happy circle ever meet again.[40]

Ultimately, six companies of infantry and several artillery units from Barbour County marched off to fight in the war, serving on battlefields from Bull Run to Appomattox. Barbour infantry units included the Louisville Blues, Clayton Guards, Pioneer Guards, Eufaula Rifles, Barbour Greys, Glennville Guards, Midway Guards, Fort Browder Roughs, Eufaula City Guards, the Eufaula Light Artillery, Dent's Battery and Kolb's Battery. At least one cavalry outfit from the county saw service as well. Many served with distinction. Four of these units, as part of the Fifteenth Alabama Infantry, would notably go on to fight with Stonewall Jackson and Robert E. Lee, eventually surrendering at Appomattox. Others—including the Eufaula Rifles, Pioneer Guards, Fort Browder Roughs and Clayton Guards—were incorporated into the First Regiment of Alabama Volunteers, organized at Glennville, which saw action throughout the western Confederacy. Men from Eufaula also played a key role in the First Battalion of Artillery, which one observer praised as the best unit of its type on either side in the war.[41]

Many of the local political leaders who spoke with such gusto about the need for a Southern Confederacy actually became among the first to offer their services in its military, and their leadership would become a special component of the Eufaula area's Civil War legacy. Three Barbour County men—Henry D. Clayton, Alpheus Baker and Cullen A. Battle—rose to the rank of general, perhaps the most of any county in Alabama. All were lawyer-politicians with no formal military training, a testimony to their position of leadership established in the antebellum era as much as their actual military abilities.

Henry D. Clayton, serving in the Alabama legislature at the time of secession, responded to the governor's call for volunteers by obtaining a leave of absence from the legislature so that he could quickly join the ranks. His wife noted that his brief return home proved just long enough to "say good-bye to loved ones, and to tell the negroes to take care of his family and to be faithful while he should be gone." In part as a result of his hurry, he had the distinction of becoming the first colonel commissioned by the Confederate government. Alpheus Baker led a Confederate unit in Vicksburg, where he was wounded, and conspicuously served at Chickamauga and Nashville. Cullen Battle became a hero for his bravery on several Eastern Theatre battlefields. These men were celebrated locally for the mere willingness to serve well before they took the field and achieved any lasting fame. One observer, remarking on the relatively advanced age of some of the first wave of Eufaula area Confederate leaders, noted at the beginning of the war that

Clayton, Bullock and John Cochran "presented a stately trio in a regiment where ninety percent of the men were less than twenty-five." Forty-one-year-old congressman James Pugh tried his hand at "stateliness" as well, joining the Eufaula Rifles as a private.[42]

As a regional transportation center, Eufaula naturally became a point of departure for companies raised in Barbour County. Several traveled from the Bluff City via steamboat to Columbus and then by rail to Montgomery, from there some moving on to Pensacola, with others being sent to the front in Virginia. These sendoffs were big events in Eufaula attended by hundreds of people. Featuring a great deal of pomp, they frequently included parades, music by bands and speeches by leading citizens. Sometimes the departures of fighting units turned into multiple-event procedures whereby the soldiers' virtue and honor were extolled in a series of parties and public gatherings. These ceremonies culminated in the presentation of banners produced by groups of local women; no sendoff was complete without the unfurling of a flag given to a local military company on behalf of "the ladies of Eufaula." Regardless of format or size, virtually every group of soldiers departing for the war from the Eufaula area ended up either at the Chattahoochee River wharf with the triumphant boarding of a steamboat or a celebratory march across the bridge into Georgia to catch a train.[43]

The sendoff for the Eufaula Rifles was perhaps the largest and among the best documented to take place in Eufaula during the war years. During the late afternoon of February 12, 1861, a large crowd assembled near the Chattahoochee River wharf downtown to see them embark via the steamboat *Ben Franklin*. Marching in formation from several blocks away with drums beating, those in attendance could hear the column long before they could actually see the company. According to a witness, the sound and its import "seemed to send a thrill through the whole assembly" and caused tears to well up in "many a mother's, wife's, sister's and friend's eyes." After the men filed past the assembled onlookers and took position along the riverbank, Captain Alpheus Baker appeared and addressed the crowd in an "eloquent touching address." James L. Pugh presented a speech after Baker, as he had been called for by the crowd. After Pugh had delivered "a few patriotic sentiments," family and friends gathered around the men of the Rifles to exchange last-minute heartfelt farewells. Soon the cry of "All aboard" rang out, and in just a few minutes, the *Ben Franklin* shoved off north for Columbus as cannons boomed. At the sight of the boat underway, the crowd burst into cheers, and hats and handkerchiefs were waved with enthusiasm. Not until the steamer was completely out of sight did the crowd disperse, "many of them with sad hearts." According to one source, some citizens actually accompanied the soldiers aboard the steamer to Columbus and then on the train as far as Montgomery.[44]

The Rifles arrived in Montgomery just in time to take part in the inauguration of Confederate president Jefferson Davis on February 18, 1861, participating in his inaugural procession. The men afterward traveled to their first post of duty in Pensacola, where upon arrival they wrote a collective letter to the citizens of the city for publication in a local paper. Addressed from the "Eufaula Rifles Parade Grounds" at Fort Barrancas, the letter expressed the unit's thanks to the citizens of Eufaula for their "continual interest in our welfare, manifested by sending us presents of those good things that contribute so much to our comfort, and at the same time giving the sweet assurance, that there are those who are interested in our fate and would drop a tear, should any fall in the approaching struggle."[45]

Most of the military units from Barbour County initially signed up for one-year terms of service, as few at that moment foresaw the war lasting any longer. Hubert Dent wrote to his wife in February 1861 from a camp near Montgomery that he had it on good authority that "we will be releaved in Six Weeks." While most expected a short war and did not contemplate a multi-year obligation, a few made a public display of being prepared to serve the length of the contest no matter the duration. With equal measures of bravado and sincerity, Edward Bullock summed up the public stance of many leading citizens when he remarked, "I am in for the war if it lasts twenty years, unless removed by that long furlough which, sooner or later, awaits all of us." Bullock's "long furlough" indeed came sooner rather than later, as he caught typhoid and died in Florida shortly after arrival, and his body was brought back somberly to Eufaula during the Christmas season of 1861. Before the first year of the war had ended, many that had flocked to the colors that that spring were already reflecting on the potential for the war to continue far in excess of their original estimate and the sacrifice that would be required to win it. The harsh realities of service in the field, the monotony and unhealthiness of camp life, the separation from family and the jarring loss of friends and acquaintances forced many to reevaluate their commitment to the Southern cause.[46]

Many of those who returned alive to Eufaula in early 1862 when their initial terms of service were up exhibited an understandable reluctance to reenlist. They were greeted as conquering heroes nonetheless. There were exuberant welcomes staged for the Pioneer Guards, Clayton Guards,

Barbour Greys and Eufaula Rifles. As the Pioneer Guards (and no doubt others) made its way into town, a cannon on the bluff fired a salute, and a band played "Home Again." Later, a party was thrown in honor of the troops at the Howard Hotel.

Once the fanfare died down, however, reenrollments proved difficult to obtain. Some units disbanded, and new ones formed in their place. In February, for example, an effort was made to reorganize the Eufaula Rifles "for the war," but only seventeen members would make the open-ended pledge. John W. Clark began to call for enlistments for a new artillery company called the Eufaula Light Artillery, which included some of the men from other units that were slow to take the field again. Meanwhile, the recruiting of replacements for those already veterans of one tour of duty began to become somewhat of a cottage industry. Henry C. Hart, among the first from Eufaula to volunteer, received a furlough to come back home and recruit replacements for his dwindling company in February 1862, for example. Local enthusiasm for the soldiers willing to serve was still in evidence, though; similar to events one year before, stores closed at 11:00 a.m. one day for a town hall meeting called to raise money to equip the new and existing companies. The Eufaula Light Artillery left town in March as those before them had a year prior, sent off with a speech followed by the music of a band as the men marched across the bridge to a train waiting on the Georgia side of the river.[47]

Gathering information about the progress of the war became a near-universal pastime in Eufaula almost before the first soldiers had left for the front. Letters to and from loved ones were for many a primary source of information, and sending and receiving them were important events in day-to-day life. While most letters traveled via the mail, some were personally delivered by people whose business or family connections might take them close to where troops were stationed. One young woman, for example, sent from a downtown Eufaula store a letter in May 1861 by way of a Dr. Wingate, who happened to be going to Pensacola, where many Eufaula troops had been posted. Others who had the means were able to arrange even more personal exchanges by visiting husbands and brothers in camp, bringing back bits of information that were widely shared. Victoria Clayton and Anna Dent were among the many Barbour County wives who traveled to visit their husbands during the war, venturing as far as Virginia to visit. In the first year of the war, Clayton recorded in her diary that she visited her husband, Henry, at his post in Pensacola and "found that several of our ladies had preceded me and were already occupying houses in the Navy

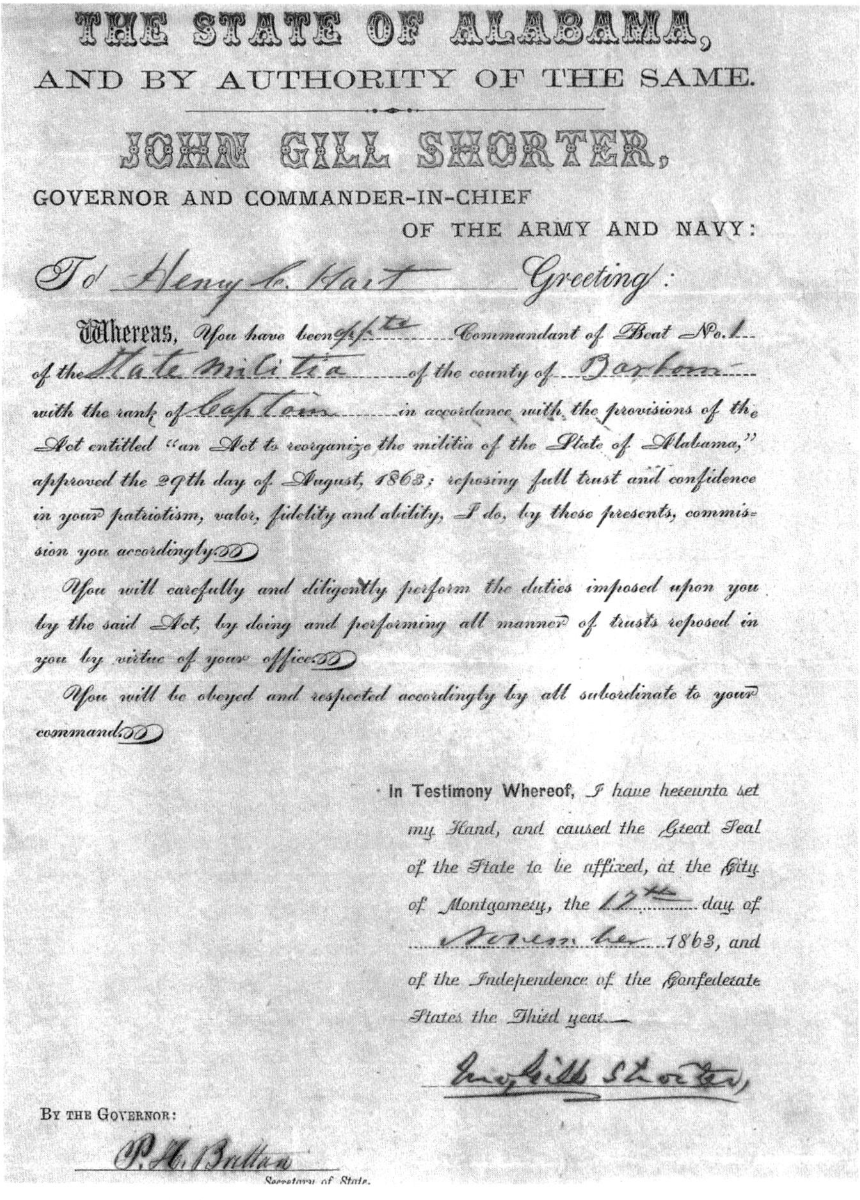

THE STATE OF ALABAMA,
AND BY AUTHORITY OF THE SAME.

JOHN GILL SHORTER,
GOVERNOR AND COMMANDER-IN-CHIEF
OF THE ARMY AND NAVY:

To *Henry C. Hart* Greeting:

Whereas, You have been *fifth* Commandant of Beat No. 1 of the *State Militia* of the county of *Barbour* with the rank of *Captain* in accordance with the provisions of the Act entitled "an Act to reorganize the militia of the State of Alabama," approved the 29th day of August, 1863; reposing full trust and confidence in your patriotism, valor, fidelity and ability, I do, by these presents, commission you accordingly.

You will carefully and diligently perform the duties imposed upon you by the said Act, by doing and performing all manner of trusts reposed in you by virtue of your office.

You will be obeyed and respected accordingly by all subordinate to your command.

In Testimony Whereof, I have hereunto set my Hand, and caused the Great Seal of the State to be affixed, at the City of Montgomery, the 12th day of November 1863, and of the Independence of the Confederate States the Third year.

Jno. Gill Shorter,

BY THE GOVERNOR:

P. H. Brittan
Secretary of State.

Commission of Eufaula resident Henry C. Hart as captain of state militia, Barbour County, signed by Governor John Gill Shorter. *Eufaula Athenaeum.*

Yard. Here we had the pleasure of seeing our husbands quite frequently." The occasional soldier returning home, whether by injury, furlough or otherwise, brought prized news that embellished accounts in the papers and provided a personal understanding of the battlefield.[48]

Indeed, from the first shots of the war to its closing campaigns, the dominant topic of conversation in the streets and parlors of Eufaula was the progress of the conflict. The telegraph certainly served as the fastest and perhaps the most dramatic source of war information; word of the first shots fired at Fort Sumter reached the city by telegraph just a few hours after the event, sparking "great excitement," according to Elizabeth Rhodes. Less visible in the public record but certainly more pervasive were the conversations of the sort she recorded as taking place about the affair in Charleston Harbor later that night at a ladies' sewing circle in which she participated. During the evening, her husband, anxious for information, went downtown "to hear the news." Such talk and efforts to find out the latest news through a variety of backchannels became part and parcel of daily life in Eufaula for the next four years. An October 1861 letter from Anna Dent to her husband, Hubert, typified many in that she expressed her thanks to him for "telling of the fight" and reminded him that she was "anxiously looking for your next letter so that I can hear the truth and see the particulars." She closed by adding that "we have seen a good deal of it in several papers," hoping that a firsthand account would embellish what she had read.[49]

However, most of the information contained in personal letters to and from the residents of Eufaula overwhelmingly concerned the routines of daily life and family events and not battles. Few events could be more poignant than the birth of a child, and many soldiers learned of these events by letter while they were away. Hubert Dent, for example, found out in a letter from Edward Young about the birth of his son, and a short time later, he received a letter from his wife describing the baby in detail. In it, she gushed, "Oh: Dearest I am so anxious for the time to come when we can go down to see you I want to be with you to see the Baby." One can only imagine the emotion with which the words were both written and received, as both knew the longing for home would not be requited for some time—indeed possibly never.

On a more lighthearted note, for some, letters from loved ones could serve as entertaining sources of information on the regions in which their loved ones were serving. Ada Dent, for example, wrote to her sister, Anna, who was at one point visiting Hubert in Pensacola, to ask her to sketch flowers she saw so that "we can see what sort they have." But most surviving correspondence indicates that Eufaulians believed that life at home paled in comparison to the perceived drama of military life. One letter summed up the thoughts of many with a simple line assuring the reader that "the times are very dull at present in Eufaula."[50]

The constant problem with war news of any kind proved to be accuracy. There was at least as much incorrect information about wartime events as accurate reporting in the newspapers. With the difficulties involved in getting correct details about developments on the front—when it could be had at all—and the multiple private and public sources through which information filtered before making its way to the streets of Eufaula, there sometimes were wildly varying perceptions of what was happening in the war. Some of this can be traced to problems inherent with wartime conditions, but some of it seemed to have been fueled at least in part by the tension-filled environment, which bred speculation and anxiety. There were multiple false alarms of Union troops in Barbour County during war. There were also, from time to time, rumors of attacks that never occurred but were certainly feared, such as the repeated rumors of a Federal attack on Apalachicola that spread throughout Eufaula on occasion.

A Federal advance upriver from the Gulf port was a great fear among local citizens, and more than once there were false alarms of Federal gunboats preparing to move up the Chattahoochee with the Bluff City in their crosshairs. On one such occasion in May 1861, the City Guards assembled and even departed via a steamboat at night to go to the aid of Apalachicola before the truth of the matter was discerned and the men were recalled to Eufaula. Should anyone have been looking for it, there was as much misinformation about Eufaula elsewhere in the country as locally. Late in the war, the *Baltimore Sun* reported that the Bluff City had fallen to Union cavalry a full week before the first soldiers even arrived in Barbour County.[51]

At times, actual events gave rise to significant but perhaps unjustified worry, such as when a local newspaper published a story about a Yankee raid elsewhere in the South that resulted in the burning of several private homes. The fear that a Yankee raid would destroy Eufaula surfaced periodically throughout the war, even though such a thing was highly unlikely until its very late stages. In such an environment of fear and worry, some in the city gave credence to superstition or simply individually decided which news to trust and which information to ignore. When a comet became visible during the war, a local diarist recorded that it was a "bad omen," foretelling of some certain tragedy for Southern arms. Rather than accept subsequent news of Confederate reverses, however, the same writer probably reflected the thoughts of many by dismissing as "full of lies" a report in the *New York Herald* commenting on Union successes.[52]

When major events occurred, their news punctuated a relatively uneventful existence at home, alternately jubilating and deflating the local populace. "The war news is daily exciting," Elizabeth Rhodes confided in her diary in the fall of 1861, betraying an early optimism in the novelty of the affair that soon gave way to the much gloomier way in which war news was received. A short summary of excerpts from her diary as the war progressed reveals the cascading pall of despair that engulfed her in her home on Randolph Avenue as the emotional blows from a steady stream of Confederate reverses and casualties took their toll. In the fall of the first year of the war, she recorded gravely that "war in its worst form is deluging our once happy land in distress and blood" and quietly contemplated "what this unjust and unholy war is costing us in Southern blood." Even more downtrodden by the midpoint of the war, she recorded after hearing of the capture of Jackson, Mississippi, that "these reverses make us feel depressed." By the winter of 1863, bemoaning that after the Confederate debacle at Chattanooga it appeared "we are to be almost overrun," she privately pleaded with God to "stop the awful war and grant that heavenly rays of peace on earth and good will to mankind on earth." One can discern a palpable frustration at the ineffectiveness of the days of fasting and prayer, periodically called for by state and national authorities, to effect a positive change in the state of affairs.[53]

In an atmosphere in which people seemed to hinge on every word from the front, it became common for the increasingly rare receipt of "good" war news, trumpeting triumphs of Southern arms, to be announced in Eufaula by the firing of "Old Punch," the cannon placed on the bluff overlooking the river (allegedly for defense). The boom of the gun no doubt sparked speculation and conversation in every corner of the city. But war news of every sort intruded into every aspect of daily life. Even in church, ministers often commented on the developments of the war or connected sermons to war-related events. Children, such as Hubert Dent's son, Eddie, sometimes brooded on the dangers faced by parents. Anna Dent related to Hubert in a letter that she told the boy that she was "afraid that the Yankees were trying to kill you. He said 'I go get my gun and kill old Yankees.'"[54]

As would be expected, however, the bulk of the correspondence to and from Eufaula residents centered on the welfare of the troops, not showdowns on the battlefield. With news of every battle that came over the wires and in the papers came the palpable and real fear that if loved ones were harmed, those at home knew that they would usually have no way of knowing until long after the guns fell silent. It would be days at best, and weeks or longer at times, if at all, that official word regarding the health of individuals might be confirmed. With the uncertainty of the mail in a war-ravaged South and the chaotic conditions on the front, alerting loved ones to the death or injury of a soldier proved more difficult and uncertain than we can imagine today. Untold numbers of local citizens first found out about injuries or deaths involving friends and family members through casualty lists published in papers, but even these appeared irregularly and were not always totally accurate or inclusive. Most people at home were forced to simply painstakingly await written word about the condition of husbands, brothers, cousins and friends from the soldiers themselves or someone who knew them. We can only imagine the tension of life in the community in the midst of such conditions. Victoria Clayton dolefully recalled that often "when all the family were wrapped in slumber and all nature hushed in the silence of night," she "walked back and forth on the colonnade until the clock would toll out the midnight hour, thinking of dear absent one."[55]

One of the most touching wartime letters from a Eufaula resident to surface is Anna Dent's letter to her husband, Hubert, in September 1863 after the Battle of Chickamauga. It captures the types of emotions and concern that kept countless local households on edge throughout the war:

Oh: My Dearest how thankful I am that you have passed through this battle safely. God has been merciful and kind to us, I have been perfectly wretched the early part of this week—In fact ever since I left you, I have been troubled and anxious, and I never prayed for you my Darling as I have the last few weeks. When we heard Tuesday morning that a terrible battle was raging in Northern Georgia—well I can never describe my feelings—and a thousand times did I think something terrible might befall you, Tuesday, Wednesday, and until noon yesterday, were days of agony to me, and night brought not rest.

I can't account for it, although I have always been anxious about you when I knew that you were in battle, yet never have I felt as I did this time, and often in imagination did I see Pa coming up, bringing some dreadful news—but thank God this terrible blow has not come upon me. My great anxiety for you, kept me from being much elated with the news of our great victory. I do hope that we have destroyed a good part of their army, but it makes me feel sad to think of the many noble lives sacrificed on that terrible battle field. Several prominent men from Columbus are killed—not a word has been heard from any one in the Eufaula Artillery. I think this is very strange as most of them have friends here. Mr. Sylvester is expected home this evening slightly wounded…

Annie had a real fit of hysteria when the dispatch came. All of us were frightened—Mamie saw Pa coming some time before our dinner hour and she went seeing after Ma who was in the back part of the house just as pale as she could be. Ma came up the passage just as Pa got in the front door, then I saw him for the first time. When I looked up he was holding both of his hands up and saying that he had a dispatch, my first thought was that you were killed and I said, Tell me what it is—Pa said Good news—Oh! My dearest I was so relieved, Annie commenced laughing and crying together, and I think most of us joined her in crying before a great while—I never had such a thankful feeling in my life—How I would like to sit down by you today and tell you all my feelings and hear you talk.

It was not to be Anna's only fearful moment during the war. A year later, during the fighting around Atlanta, an incorrect report of her husband's death reached her after someone had misidentified him in a letter to a loved one in the Eufaula area. He wrote to her afterward with a touch of humor that he was "very well Honey—but poor."[56]

Many others, of course, were not so fortunate. The war provided a seemingly unending list of casualties from battlefield fighting and disease and infection in camps and hospitals that made many hearts "almost burst with grief." Virtually everybody in the town and county knew somebody who had lost a loved one in the war through one of these means. One Barbour County resident remembered that she had a neighbor who had four sons killed in fighting in Tennessee in different battles. Another recorded how she "wept with a widow bereft of her only son and child, who had died in a hospital near Richmond…she told us…her last words to him as she held his hand had been, 'My son, remember it is just as near heaven in Virginia as it is here in our home in Alabama.'"

The emotions that racked the homes of so many local families who suffered such losses defy description not only because our society has never again suffered loss on the scale of that which took place during the Civil War but also due to the simple fact that so few of their stories are recorded in any form. For every one story that survives, even secondhand through the pen of a neighbor's diary, there were dozens of others that will never be chronicled.[57]

Chapter 4

"These Days of War and Blockade Tried Our Souls"

On July 4, 1861, Elizabeth Rhodes made a simple notation in her diary that poignantly revealed how much had changed so quickly in Eufaula since the war began. "How differently the day is spent now and several years ago," she recorded, noting reflectively that "[i]t was for many, many years a national holiday." Much had changed indeed, for wartime Eufaula was a different place in virtually every way from the city its residents had been accustomed to prior to the beginning of hostilities. The war exerted a tremendous impact on the domestic economy and altered the rhythms of life in Eufaula on every level, producing a melancholy among residents about their situation that is tangible in diaries and correspondence. The formerly buzzing downtown was quiet and steamboat whistles relatively rarely heard. Domestic economic hardship would be one of the defining hallmarks of the town's wartime experience.[58]

There had been hopes that this would not be the case. As a prominent trading town a relatively short distance from the new Confederate republic's first capital, Eufaula had naturally figured into its early financial plans. Shortly after secession, Alabama governor A.B. Moore quickly set about trying to get the finances of the state in order, making arrangements with five large banks throughout the state, including the Eastern National Bank in Eufaula, so that "they should, if required by the Legislature, furnish to the State a loan of $1,000,000 in specie or its equivalent." He offered as his rationale that despite the chaotic financial environment in which several banks temporarily had suspended activities, those selected as potential

War-era note issued by Eufaula merchant Thomas J. Cannon. *Eufaula Athenaeum.*

lenders were "able to sustain themselves though the crisis, and…there can be no question of their solvency." Many likewise entertained the notion that Eufaula's position as a regional center of trade precluded economic failure. In a show of confidence in the Confederate cause, local banker John McNab had his Eastern Bank designated a Confederate depository office, where bonds could be issued. The depths of the economic crisis into which the war plummeted the city and region took even the most informed by surprise.[59]

Economic activity in the city declined quickly and precipitously once the war began. Statistics are lacking due to the paucity of records with which to accurately measure economic activity both before and during the war, but by every account, trade slowed to a crawl. One gauge of the economic health of the city, newspaper advertisements, reveals increasingly desperate merchants who switched from the standard prewar practice of extending credit to customers to demanding cash at the time of sale. Shortly after the war commenced, for example, merchant John McNaughton asked for those who had bought from him with promises to pay upon the sale of their cotton crops the coming winter to pay up immediately. Despite closing his notice in the *Eufaula Express* with "God Save the Confederate States," the stipulation obviously had less to do with patriotic feeling than a fear that normal business conditions would soon be, if not already were, drastically interrupted. J.A. Hunter, a bookseller and stationer, similarly ran an advertisement in a local paper under the heading, "I Am Forced to Do It" stating candidly that "owing to the unsettled state of the country, and the pressure of the

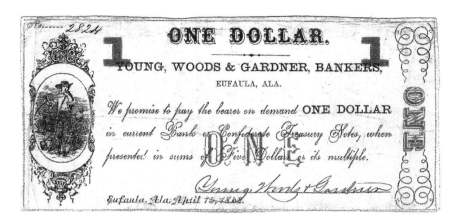

War-era note issued by the private Eufaula bank of Young, Woods and Gardner. *Eufaula Athenaeum*.

times, I am compelled to adopt the CASH SYSTEM exclusively." Elsewhere, John McNab and Son posted a "Special Notice" in the *Spirit of the South* explaining that "the stringency of MONEY MATTERS compels us to demand in future CASH for all GOODS furnished."

Eufaula's architectural legacy, much of it a testament to the remarkable local craftsman George Whipple, itself tells the story in a physical and obvious way. The city abounds in historic homes, virtually all built in the decades before and after the war; there are almost no structures surviving in Eufaula that are known to have been built from 1861 to 1865.[60]

From the outset of the war, it seemed as if the context of every business transaction and purchase had suddenly changed. Anticipating shortages of supplies at the beginning of the war and uncertain of their future livelihoods, people from throughout the countryside crowded into town to stock up on provisions and put their financial affairs in order. At the same time, a smaller out-migration of residents occurred, as those from elsewhere, especially those hailing from the North, began to make plans to return home as the crisis loomed. Schools closed as instructors, many Northern-born, returned to their homes, and parents kept children at home waiting for the situation to be sorted out. Businesses reconsidered extending further long-term credit and began to hike prices on goods, expecting serious disruptions with Northern suppliers. The situation gradually grew acute as basic necessities became more difficult to obtain. At the height of the war, some local residents were reported to be near starvation. "The country is destitute of clothing, meat, Coffee and but little Salt," John Horry Dent noted with alarm. "Suffering

Note issued by the Eastern National Bank. *Eufaula Athenaeum*.

will be inevitable for a time to come…Heaven knows what I am to do for Negro clothing and meat this year."[61]

Purchases naturally became limited to what was immediately necessary, and then only if the increasingly difficult to obtain hard cash was available. One local resident wrote despairingly, "The war has suspended business. Trade is confined only to necessities and economy is the order of the day." Allusions to local business activity as not just slow but "almost suspended" abound in the accounts of wartime Eufaula. Many businesses failed in such an environment, and city government was strained to its limit. Elizabeth Rhodes observed forlornly in the middle of the war that "our streets and business houses present quite a deserted appearance since this war commenced." Local tax revenues declined rapidly with the cessation of normal activities, and consequently essential services became harder to provide. Taxation by the Confederate government, both in cash and in kind, placed an enormous burden on families throughout the region. For much of the war, citizens were required to give one-tenth of all agricultural production to the Confederate government. Victoria Clayton remembered how "after delivering the government tithe, and sharing with our home ones, the crop rarely lasted till another harvest." The Confederate quartermaster stationed in town, whose responsibility it was to requisition supplies for the Confederate government, could not have been an especially popular person.[62]

There were many reasons for the economic slowdown, most having to do generally with difficult wartime conditions across the South. Cotton prices, long the bellwether economic indicator for Eufaula and the surrounding region, plummeted to a mere seven cents per pound, and cotton in

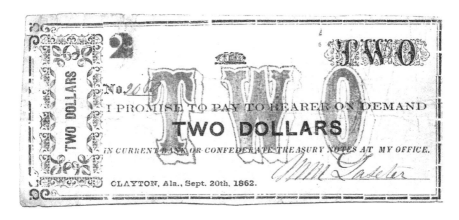

Two-dollar note issued by a merchant in Clayton. *Eufaula Athenaeum.*

Confederate Treasury note issued in Eufaula. *Eufaula Athenaeum.*

Apalachicola, unable to be shipped, was worth only ten cents on the dollar. As business proprietors of military age were called into the ranks, their establishments were often run under most dire circumstances by widows, wives and children who frequently had little business experience. Manpower and transportation were generally in short supply.

A chief culprit of the economic havoc was undoubtedly the blockade of the Gulf of Mexico port of Apalachicola, Florida, by the Union navy. Shut off from a sea outlet for cotton that doubled as a primary supply route of consumer goods, Eufaula was suddenly isolated from a large portion of its customary trading network. "We were caged up like a besieged city," observed one local resident with only a degree of exaggeration. Wagon routes and the railroad on the Georgia side of the river that linked the Chattahoochee to Savannah became the city's only practical commercial outlets for much of the war. With Savannah likewise blockaded and supply disruptions in every commercial artery, business activity in Eufaula virtually stopped.[63]

The river was not entirely devoid of traffic, though. A few steamers, such as the *Indian, Munnerlyn, Uchee, William H. Young* and the *Shamrock*, continued running between Columbus and towns in northern Florida at intervals throughout the war. Wartime advertisements listed the *Indian* as leaving Columbus Sundays at 6:00 a.m. bound for "Riccoe's Bluff" along the southern stretches of the Apalachicola River. It was still running that route in the final months of the war as much as three times per week. Oceangoing steamers laden with civilian goods did infrequently slip past the blockade to have their cargo transferred onto steamboats and shipped upriver. The boats that did run somewhat regularly ultimately ended up carrying as much merchandise for the military as civilian trade. As much of this material, often smuggled, was bound for Columbus, Eufaula maintained its position as an important waypoint between the river's Gulf outlet and its head of navigation. But steamboat arrivals and departures were much fewer, and dramatically lower volumes of goods were traded at the city's wharf during the war.[64]

When shipments of supplies did arrive in town, the event was major news. Parthenia Hague recounted in her memoirs the excitement brought about in the community upon the occasion that a steamer docked in Eufaula with scarce fabrics and a variety of other supplies that had successfully been run through the blockade. "Mr. G. ordered Ben to harness up the horses, and we were driven to Eufaula, not to buy, but simply to have a look at these imports. Sure enough, on the shelves in the store that had long lain empty, there were tastefully disposed a few bolts of English prints, some ladies' straw hats, a bolt or two of fine bleached stuff, some calico, and a few pair of ladies' shoes. These were the magnets which had drawn us eleven miles!" She recorded that she did purchase a small amount of fabric, for which she admitted she paid dearly, but noted that its appearance caused a stir at home. "As soon as it was noised about in that quiet settlement that we had new store-bought calicoes," she recorded, "all paid us a visit in order that they might see how a new print looked amidst so much home-woven cloth."[65]

The steamboat *Shamrock* was built during the war to supply the Confederate Naval Iron Works in Columbus. This image, taken shortly after the end of the war, shows the boat at Apalachicola loaded with cotton. *State Archives of Florida, Florida Memory.*

Word of mouth would have probably been sufficient, but stores that obtained prized merchandise for sale such as that which lured Hague and her employer's family quickly let it be known in the local papers. In June 1863, for example, a local merchant touted that he recently had obtained "goods from Charleston… including camphor, rhubarb, ginger." A few days later, a grocer named Godwin announced that he had just received "tobacco, rice, peaches, pepper, bar soap, copperas, needles, and envelopes," likely from the same shipment.

Yet despite shortages of supplies, difficulties of transportation and a shrinking market of customers, the types of goods available in the hit-and-miss supply chain fueled largely by blockade running might be surprising. Eufaulians could still obtain a "metallic burial case" at Ramser's Furniture Warehouse and tobacco from Virginia on the eve of the Battle of Gettysburg, for example. These announcements would have been met with enthusiasm by the steadily shrinking crowds that could afford them, for inflation was ravaging the economy as much as the blockade. John Horry Dent bemoaned in 1864 that bacon was sixty cents per pound and sugar an incredible twelve dollars per pound. He had reason to complain; just two years earlier, prevailing prices within the region for sugar had been as low as fifty cents per pound, and even lower than that prior to the war. Elizabeth Rhodes noted bitterly that in December 1863 she had to pay the exorbitant price of twenty dollars each for three pigs, for which before the war she would have expected to pay just one dollar per head.[66]

Blockade Raised !
McGINTY & SMITH,
JUST RECEIVED from CHARLESTON,
and now offer for sale, the following : :

Castor Oil,
Calomel,
Epsom Salts,
Gum Camphor,
Pulv. Rhubarb,
Race Ginger,
Black Pepper,
Extract Logwood,
Bar Soap,
Wolfe's Scheidam Snapps,
Sulphate Morphine and Quinine, and many
other indispensible articles. Call early and
supply yourselves, or you may lose the chance.
Eufaula, June 17, 1862.   1 tf.

Announcement of the arrival of goods obtained via a blockade runner. *Alabama Department of Archives and History.*

For a select few Eufaula businessmen, wartime business proved brisk despite the general downturn in the economy. Some, like Edward Young, who had brother William's mill in Columbus as an outlet for his cotton, had special advantages. With its large military-industrial complex that rivaled Richmond's, Columbus businesses constantly advertised their need for wool and cotton during war. While the situation was exceptional, a few locals did benefit. Others held on to their wealth by sheer force of will. There is the story, for example, of banker John McNab, who, dressed in shabby clothes, allegedly traveled to Mobile and then by steerage on to Liverpool carrying cotton receipts for thousands of dollars unredeemable locally. He reportedly used the cash, concealed on himself as he traveled back, to operate the beleaguered Eastern National Bank.[67]

If there was any common denominator in the economic reverses that affected all classes of Eufaula society, it lay in the fact that the war forced people to become more self-sufficient. Empty store shelves, dwindling supplies, inflation and a scarcity of cash combined to force a new mode of living for many that demanded inventiveness in fulfilling needs. The situation did not come about as a total surprise to Eufaulians. Early on in the war, most thoughtful observers began to realize that the ordeal might be long in duration, and those who understood the basic underpinnings of the Southern economy braced themselves for some degree of financial upheaval. Locals were well aware of the industrial disadvantage under which the South labored and realized that the manufactured goods and foodstuffs they bought from elsewhere might soon become difficult to replace. "We have too long relied on the Yankees for nearly almost everything," noted Elizabeth Rhodes. Parthenia Hague likewise acknowledged that "[u]p to the beginning of the war we had been dependent on the North for almost everything eaten and worn." Rather than dwell in despair, local citizens met the crisis with ingenuity.[68]

Almost immediately, they expanded the range of crops grown locally. With the cotton markets in disarray and seeking to provide themselves both a new cash crop and a measure of self-sufficiency, many Barbour County planters soon began to plant wheat, rye, rice, oats and peanuts in earnest. Others attempted for the first time to grow rice and sugar cane in available moist patches of land, and home-fashioned rice mills sprang up here and there in the area. This crop diversification took place fairly quickly; one person claimed to have raised almost all the provisions needed by his family by the second year of the war. Those who did not turn their efforts toward self-sufficiency and continued to focus on cotton production were viewed by some as profiteers and not true Southern patriots. Even before the war, Eufaula newspapers expressed frustration that planters were having huge supplies of foodstuffs shipped into the Chattahoochee Valley rather than grow more themselves in 1860. The wartime attention to growing more food staples is perhaps best demonstrated by the fact that as money grew scarce during the war, corn came to be used by some as a commodity. Planter John Horry Dent recorded ears being traded for newspapers, provisions, medical services and even used to hire a tutor. But growing more food for themselves was just the beginning for the residents of the Eufaula area.[69]

A great majority of Parthenia Hague's account of wartime life is devoted to chronicling the myriad ways self-sufficiency manifested itself in her household and in her neighborhood once the trading supply train ran off the tracks. According to her book, Eufaula-area citizens spent a great deal of time creating substitutes for articles they could no longer obtain regularly. They made their own flour from homegrown wheat, syrup and sugar from watermelons, coffee from okra and sweet potatoes and tea from sassafras root or holly tree leaves, and they also used corncob ashes as a substitute for baking soda. They scraped the floors of smokehouses and boiled the dirt to recover precious salt. They crafted homemade leather from slaughtered cow skins and fashioned swine skin shoes when brogans could not be bought. One slave owner sent a slave to work in a shoe shop in Clayton to learn to make shoes owing to the difficulty in obtaining them elsewhere. Locals extracted homemade dyes from a variety of roots, barks and berries and used rusted metal to make copperas to help the dyes adhere to cloth. People made wooden buttons from seeds and burned cottonseed and peanut oil instead of kerosene for lights. They reused shoe soles with homemade uppers and kept poultry in the backyard for meat and eggs with renewed focus.[70]

Fashioning substitutes for scarce items of all sorts became a virtual pastime in the Eufaula area. "The woods...were also our drug stores," one person remembered. Bark and berry extracts were used as medicine and poppies cultivated for opium—Parthenia Hague reminisced nostalgically that "the soporific influence of this drug was not excelled by that of the imported article." Newspapers frequently carried articles advising readers on how to make substitutes for a wide variety of everyday household products that were suddenly in short supply. The *Spirit of the South* in 1861 ran an article advising readers on how to manufacture a substitute for coffee from garden beets "in these days of blockades, when coffee is scarce, prices high, and in many places none to be had at any price." Foregoing such mysterious alchemy, another writer urged readers to simply save used coffee grounds, dry them and then regrind to produce a passable, if weaker, coffee because it was obvious that the cherished beans would be in short supply for some time.[71]

With imports of finished goods virtually halted, area citizens also learned to make more of their own clothing. Sewing societies were formed throughout the county and spinning bees held to produce necessary items. Every home seemed to have had a spinning wheel, and female slaves on virtually every plantation were put to work spinning thread. But thrift and ingenuity extended beyond traditional modes of domestic manufacture. Women were seen wearing hats of plaited palm leaves, straw or corn shucks soaked in water and then woven.[72]

Locals seemed to take patriotic pride in having accomplished what they did in conserving precious resources, fashioning substitutes for those that could not be had and generally doing with less. For some, it seemed to purify the cause for which their nation fought. Parthenia Hague wrote somewhat melodramatically after being reduced to wearing hogskin shoes that this very act provided a sort of moral justification for the Southern cause and proved that her family indeed was "willing to immolate ourselves on the altar of our Southern Confederacy." Others celebrated their own practicality in more understated tones. "I am now writing by a candle of our own moulding," wrote John Horry Dent in a wartime letter, "and I have made a loom, spinning wheels &c to embark at once in domestic manufacturers...The socks I daily ware [sic] is of Mrs. Dents knitting, and she says she will not stop until we are clothed in part out of our looms." Dent believed that self-sufficiency and thrift of this sort were necessary for both immediate reasons and also served a purpose toward a higher calling. He noted as if chastened and awakened that "reformation was needed, for before the war we had become an indecent arrogant people...Our daughters now must go to the looms instead of piano forts [sic] and our young men instead of fast clerks to something more useful and practical. With this great evil, a large amount of good must also come from this war."[73]

Communities came together to share limited resources. One person noted that "in case one was so fortunate as to secure a sugar mill with iron cylinders, it used to go the rounds of its immediate vicinity, as the portable threshers did." Dwindling supplies of valued staples such as flour and coffee were apparently not hoarded so much as saved so that they could be savored. "It was quite amusing to hear the neighbors as they met in social gatherings, or perhaps when separating from service at church, press their friends to come and see them, or come and have dinner," remembered one diarist, "for we have got a barrel of flour." The shortages did not stop efforts to contribute needed supplies and comfort items to the troops, though. Throughout the war, the women of Eufaula worked diligently to provide through voluntary "sewing circles" and a local Soldiers Relief Society an endless supply of socks, shirts, pants, coats and, at times, even foodstuffs to the men in the ranks to supplement an unpredictable and inadequate Confederate provisioning system. Females of every age apparently participated; even eleven-year-old Mollie Hyatt knitted a scarf to send to Virginia along with dozens of others produced by local women. Others sent more specifically military-related items, such as John Horry Dent, who sent his son a revolver by mail when he entered service in the Confederate navy.[74]

Rationing was made all the more difficult by the fact that as supplies dwindled, the population actually grew. A large number of refugees, seeking relief from life on the front lines in Alabama, Georgia and Mississippi especially, made their way to Eufaula during the war. Many of these people were provided for through the hospitality of local citizens and fed and clothed through the generosity of the community, and many Eufaula ladies volunteered serving the poor and the displaced. Most, however, stayed with relatives or friends, some so long that they became full-fledged members of local society. Not all the new arrivals were indigent, however. John Horry Dent, who was kin to outspoken political figure Robert Barnwell Rhett of South Carolina, late in the war welcomed the Rhetts and several of their slaves to his Barbour County plantation when they fled before General William T. Sherman's advance into the Carolinas in the spring of 1865. How many others arrived in Eufaula under similar circumstances may never be known.[75]

Of course, pride, hospitality and patriotic spirit could only buoy spirits of weary citizens for so long. There was in the end very real financial strain and physical discomfort involved in having to do without things to which people were accustomed. "Now and then, it is true, a steamer would run the blockade, but the few articles in the line of merchandise that reached us served only as a reminder of the outside world and of our once great plenty, now almost forgotten, and also more forcibly to remind us that we must depend upon our own ingenuity to supply the necessities of existence." Parthenia Hague remembered candidly that "as the novelty of carding and spinning wore off, we often grew weary in our strife."[76]

The stress associated with wartime hardship is poignantly detailed in the writings of local citizens. "These days of war and blockade tried our souls," remembered Victoria Clayton. "Alas! How little did we think we would eventually be called on to submit, and to give up the results of our labor for all these years of our young lives, and in old age to feel privation!" Tensions dwelled on the minds of local citizens and weighed heavily on their hearts to the point that a forlorn gloom seemed to hang in the air. Elizabeth Rhodes was grief-stricken by the thought that "around many firesides in the South," there were "vacant chairs....whose occupants have fallen on the bloody fields." "Black Roll...from Alpha to Omega. Battles, Murder & desolation the order of the day. Heaven and Earth seems Convulsed," recorded John Horry Dent. One Eufaula resident recorded on New Years Day 1863 that a "new year dawns with bright sunshine, but deep shadows have fallen upon many once happy homes, and yet 'cruel war' has hardly begun her horrid work of blood and carnage." The day, formerly an occasion for community celebrations, passed with "no festivities." So difficult were things at home that in John Gill Shorter's failed bid for reelection as governor, war weariness prevailed to an extent that he failed to carry even Barbour County. People were heartily sick of the war by its third summer.[77]

But not every day of the war was dismal in the Eufaula area. Diaries of locals reveal that citizens kept up a relatively active social life despite the circumstances, regularly visiting friends and attending a number of parties, dances, lectures, concerts and other amusements that relieved the strain that almost daily asserted its presence. Elizabeth Rhodes made a point of noting that she had happily gotten a chance to attend a concert by "Blind Tom," the celebrated savant slave musician from Columbus, and "was never so highly entertained in my life." Habitually eloquent Parthenia Hague remembered in reflection that despite the chaos of war, there were times "in our quiet valley, which, we were vain enough to believe, rivaled the far-famed Vale of Cashmere, everything moved on the even tenor of its way."

Newspaper accounts show that even late in the war, the trains just across the river in Georgia ran a somewhat normal schedule, and farmers, economic disaster notwithstanding, were plagued by the usual inconveniences such as the occasional strayed mule. Students still learned their lessons in school—only, as Mollie Hyatt noted, instruction in geography now required learning the borders of the *Confederate* states. There were still festive barbecues held in town for special events. Children still visited friends to play and celebrate birthdays. Locals welcomed friends in private homes, even if the feasts featured not the usual prewar plenty but "all the delicacies the Confederacy afforded." The Eufaula Female Institute and Union Female College still held commencements. People still attended church and heard sermons convicting them of the same bad behaviors as before the war. One Eufaula citizen wrote to her husband in the ranks almost humorously that he "ought to have heard the sermon Mr. Cottrell preached yesterday, he gave it to tobacco chewers and smokers, and the use of tobacco generally. I agreed with him fully and I think you would too. I don't believe there is one of his male members who does not chew—there sat Pa chewing all the while as he usually does, but he seemed very much amused."[78]

People still lived and died along the river, with sickness and accidents claiming lives just as surely as bullets. A Mr. Jordan committed suicide in January 1861 "while in a fit of mental aberration." A young man named Henry Daniel drowned trying to cross the Chattahoochee in a small boat. Smallpox, a frequent and insidious health threat before, during and after the war, broke out in the summer of 1864 and caused much alarm in the city. Letters to and from soldiers were replete with details on the sickness and health of friends and relatives, and private diaries record the distress and heartbreak that accompanied the not-infrequent deaths of citizens, especially children, from a variety of the illnesses that carried off so many during that era. The war simply intruded into life in ways that made all other things somehow temporarily subsumed. While signal war-related events are naturally the most remarked on, available records reveal that locals demonstrated a focused resilience to a variety of trying circumstances exacerbated by the conflict throughout the crisis.[79]

Nowhere was this resilience more evident than within the area's slave population. We can never know the true feelings, thoughts and conversations of the enslaved residents of Eufaula and Barbour County during the Civil War. We can only imagine the anxiety with which they followed the progress of the events that were the subject of conversation everywhere around them, as well as the certainty that they knew they portended change. Exactly what type of alteration in their circumstance might occur was no clearer to them than to the area's white population, however. If anything, it may have been even less so. It must have felt as if the entire world the slaves knew was inexorably advancing toward a precipice that might truly result in a cataclysmic upheaval that would turn all upside down, and they were far from certain that it might better their station. Considering that station, though, it was a risk they were happily willing to take.

Slavery had a long history in Barbour County by the time of the Civil War. The earliest American settlers in the area brought their slaves with them in the 1820s. By the outbreak of the war, as elsewhere in the South, the institution of slavery had become a cornerstone of the local economic and social structure. Few in the Eufaula area could have imagined life without slavery regardless of their opinion of the institution, as it manifested itself in virtually every aspect of daily life. Slaves harvested the crops that were brought to local markets, loaded and unloaded cargo onto the steamboats at the wharf in Eufaula, attended the homes that locals lived in or visited, transported provisions purchased in local stores back to plantations and were seen in the streets, roads and virtually all public places. Even in a deferential role in which they clearly formed the bottom rung on the social ladder, slaves were an integral part of the community's social fabric.

According to local legend, one of Eufaula's primary slave markets, the spot where men and women were traded openly as commodities, is located in the median of Broad Street between Randolph and Orange Avenues. It says much about the society at the time that its exact location goes virtually unmentioned as either unimportant, so commonly known it did not merit consideration or perhaps so shameful locals would prefer it overlooked, in period accounts of life in the city. Consequently, the exact spot of this evocative location has been forgotten. There were surely many such locations in the area that have been lost to time. The sixth-most populous county in the state in 1860, more than half of Barbour County's population was enslaved.[80]

With intense day-to-day contact unavoidable, genuine bonds formed between many whites and blacks that were rooted in a great degree of shared experience, even though their positions in society were very different. These bonds influenced the way the war was experienced and remembered in complex ways that cannot be reduced to simple phrases. Regardless of how they may have viewed one another privately, slaves and owners often literally grew up together, celebrated the same happy events and experienced the sickness and death of loved ones together. Matilda Pugh Daniel, for example, a slave of leading political figure James L. Pugh, worked in his house daily and played with his children. She remembered in an interview in her later years how she played "injuns in de woods, an' buil' dams down on de creek an' swing in de yard" with the Pugh children. Daniel was even married in the parlor of her master's home wearing a dress that belonged to his wife. Lizzie Hill, a slave in Barbour County during the war, recalled later that she "had two little mistises 'bout as old as me, and I played wid dem all de time and slep' on a pallet in dey room ev'y night. Dey slep' on de big bed. My clothes was jes' as good and clean as deyrn, and I et what dey et."

When particularly beloved individual bondsmen became seriously ill, they were frequently the subject of concern and prayer similar to that bestowed on white community members. When a longtime slave of her family passed away during the war, for example, Elizabeth Rhodes remarked that she at last had reluctantly reconciled herself to "the will of God" because "we all feel very much attached to him." Accounts of life during the era abound with tales of gatherings for barbecues and slave weddings in which everyone in attendance, white and black, seem to have enjoyed themselves. Owners expressed genuine affection for certain slaves, and in later interviews, some slaves professed to have held some former owners in high regard. Certainly, there are degrees of self-service to be sorted through in understanding these comments, but not all of these positive reminiscences of individual relationships can be dismissed as contrived.[81]

This does not, of course, mean that slaves were happy with their situation or that owners really thought of them on any level as their equal. Regardless of the warm memories of interactions that manifested

Top: Matilda Pugh Daniel. *Library of Congress.*

Bottom: Lizzie Hill. *Library of Congress.*

themselves in nostalgic accounts of life during the era by slave owners or in probing interviews of suspicious and careful former slaves by unfamiliar whites, the institution of slavery was a detestable business whose very premise rested on the idea of race-based inequality. The same records that show whites choosing only to remember a scattered few happy times also demonstrate a calculating commodification of slaves and show that seeming kindness is best understood through the veil of economic self-interest. Eufaulian Henry C. Hart, for example, wrote to his wife from the field during the war advising her that not for comfort or humanity but to avoid illness, and hence a decline in productivity among their slaves, the "negroes must be well clothed at any cost" after she presumably questioned the proper amount of expenditure required for slave clothing. Others were more explicit in the rationale for perceived kindness. When a slave on the Garland plantation named Jim fell sick, Parthenia Hague remembered tellingly that his master cautioned all to "be careful of Jim, and see to it that he lacks for nothing; if he dies, I've lost one thousand dollars."[82]

The war upset the traditional dynamics of the area's slave-based labor system in profound ways long before emancipation. One of the most noteworthy changes from the perspective of slaves would be the unprecedented absence of owner oversight. With so many of the men of age for military service away during the war, many plantations were left to the care of trusted slaves. Victoria Clayton remembered that her family had left their plantation "entirely in the care of negroes...not a white face was on the plantation. Everything had been entrusted to old Joe, the foreman, and Nancy, his wife," with whom she conducted periodic inspections of the plantation. Most area plantations seem to have continued on with a degree of normalcy, but with supervision becoming more lax, it is no surprise that there was an increase in runaways and a decline in production during the war. Perhaps one of the most unique ways the war intruded into the institution of slavery, however, was by its demands on slave labor. Some slaves accompanied their masters when they first left for the war as bodyservants or cooks. Henry C. Hart of Eufaula, for example, had a slave named Simon sent to the front line to cook for his company when the white cook they had hired proved unequal to the task. Others were forced to work on Confederate defenses around the state. Barbour County slaves were pressed into service on the defenses at Mobile and at other points on occasion.[83]

Bondsmen, of course, viewed the war very differently from the area's white population. Interviews with former slaves conducted by the Works

Wallace Comer with his bodyservant. *Rob Schaffeld.*

Progress Administration in the 1930s (the Slave Narratives project) offer some glimpses into just how differently. Even though these sources are flawed for a variety of reasons, they nevertheless provide us with some of the very few clues as to slave thoughts during the time. Gus Askew, a slave born in nearby Henry County who moved to Eufaula during the war, remembered the celebration in the town when news of secession came over the wires. Speaking candidly, he stated pointedly "dat was one time when de ban' was playin' and flags was flyin' dat us lil' niggers didn't get no joy outen it."

It is widely known and well documented in other locations that the close-knit slave community kept abreast of events during the war to a far greater degree than might be suspected. Whether through eavesdropping on the conversations of whites or simply listening to talk on the streets and trading houses, slaves across the South usually knew almost as much as the white community about the progress of the war. They certainly discussed these events and what they meant in private. Firsthand evidence of how this grapevine of information played out in the Eufaula

Gus Askew. *Library of Congress.*

area has yet to be found, however, and will probably never be discovered. How many slaves such as Byrd Day (who read the Bible to his fellow bondsmen) existed is unknown, but there surely were others like him who knew how to read and understood his people's situation with unusual clarity.[84]

The bulk of the scattered references contained in the Slave Narratives to wartime conversations among slaves center on the arrival of Union troops in Eufaula in the closing days of the conflict. Several slaves remembered the commotion caused when Union troops appeared in April 1865. Many would be charged with hiding the valuables of owners in whatever spots they could find. Most certainly welcomed the sight of the blue-clad troops and the end of slavery that their arrival foretold. Their first encounters with their would-be liberators were not always remembered fondly, though. Some, such as Theodore Stewart, recalled that he witnessed Yankees burn everything on one plantation except the slave cabin, but this seeming gesture of favoritism rang hollow when the soldiers proceeded to then take "all de horses and everything us had to eat." Others reported that they were robbed by occupying troops. One history of Eufaula recounts an anecdote about a local slave in which Union soldiers forced him to surrender $2.50 for a certificate that he believed entitled him to "40 acres and a mule." Illiterate, he only belatedly discovered that he had been duped into purchasing a worthless scrap of paper.

Even if some did find out that Yankees could mistreat them as well as the Southerners they were accustomed to, all slaves celebrated the coming of freedom. Some were told that they were free by solemn masters, others realized the situation and simply stopped work or left their former homes altogether. Regardless, the realization that change had come was profound indeed. Theodore Stewart recounted for an interviewer late in life with some degree of satisfaction how when the Yankees arrived in Barbour County, "ol' Marster went off somewhar...I don't 'member where; an' when he come back he had to live in one of de nigger cabins 'til he could build a house." He noted wryly upon reflection that "de new one wasn't big lak de old one."[85]

Chapter 5
"Positively Needed in the Valley of the Chattahoochee"

Although the war intruded into every aspect of daily life in Eufaula, the city had the good fortune of remaining on its periphery, militarily speaking, until its closing days. This fact notwithstanding, Eufaulians did take steps to prepare for its defense in case of an unlikely emergency. Actual construction of defensive positions proved minimal—a powder magazine supposedly was built on the bluff overlooking the river, presumably to supply the laughably inadequate artillery that could have been brought to bear on an approaching warship. Residents of the town during the war years would fondly remember "Old Punch" and another, larger gun as local landmarks of sorts during the war—but, tellingly, not because they managed to turn away any Federal fleets. "Punch" was fired whenever good news regarding Confederate arms was received, becoming more of a tourist attraction and information source than a protector. Had an attack actually occurred, the front lines of Eufaula's defenders would have been not gun emplacements or fortifications but rather those men still in town too young, too old or physically unable to serve in the ranks as regular troops.[86]

Early on in the conflict, some of these men had been organized into a reserve corps that could be called on in case of emergency. As early as the spring of 1862, stores were closing early so that older men in town, many employed in businesses and virtually all those capable of bearing arms that remained in town, could organize into a company of minutemen as first responders should an attack occur. A Eufaula "Home Reserves" unit later formed that contained a number of businessmen too old to serve in regular units—Edward Young and his partners Clayton R. Woods, Colin Gardner and John McNab were included. Lest there be any doubt that the unit contained men who were physically unable to serve in regular units, two younger enrollees were listed as having "crippled" hands. This organization became the Eufaula company of the State Guard, commanded by John Hardy. Little is known about how often they met or drilled, but they evidently did practice their marksmanship on occasion.

Governor John Gill Shorter praised the unit as a "very efficient operation" of "sharpshooters" in a letter to Confederate secretary of war James A. Seddon. He mentioned the men because he wanted to impress on the secretary that units such as the State Guard were "positively needed in the valley of the Chattahoochee" and asked that they continue to be allowed to volunteer for state instead of Confederate service. Shorter wrote that he feared that with the scarce population of west Florida and the counties of southeast Alabama, already stripped of men and resources, even a small Union raid might be able to lay waste to the area. His concern could naturally be viewed as part political posturing for local friends, but he and other leaders held genuine concern about the military preparedness of the region. The area featured few major population centers, and with so much of its manpower away in the ranks of the Confederate army, it lay wholly unprotected from a cavalry strike. Indeed, even basic communication proved difficult with the severe manpower shortages the region experienced. The superintendent of the Columbus telegraph office insisted during the war that if three of his operators—two at Eufaula and one at Columbia, Alabama—were not relieved from conscription in the army, the line to Tallahassee would have to be abandoned.[87]

As a city whose very existence was intertwined with the rise and fall of the Chatthaooochee Valley cotton trade, Eufaula keenly felt the effects of the Federal blockade of the river's Gulf outlet at Apalachicola, Florida. The primary purpose of the Union effort was to cut off river traffic at the Gulf's third-largest cotton port and damage the region's economy. The blockade began on June 11, 1861, with arrival of the USS *Montgomery* and the reading of a proclamation. The Confederates did their best to prevent some of the valuable navigational items around the blockaded port from falling into Union hands, sending a number of buoys and some important lighthouse equipment from Apalachicola upriver to Eufaula for safekeeping.

River traffic slowed immediately. Just as quickly, if not more so, those living along the river began to formulate plans to break the blockade. Most plans were nothing more than pipe dreams, but authorities did invest in a fantastic plot to run an ironclad being built at the naval yards in Columbus down the river and scatter the blockading ships. Construction delays, manpower shortages, logistical difficulties and, ultimately, the extreme shallowness of the river itself combined to negate the plan before it ever seriously got started. More effective were attempts to run the blockade from the Gulf and bring in supplies to Apalachicola. Exactly how many shipments of goods made it past Union patrols and upriver is difficult to ascertain. The odds were good enough and the profits sufficiently high to ensure the continuation of the practice throughout the war. Steamers of light draft, able to get in and out of the port, passed undetected from time to time, and five are known to have made the run successfully in November 1862 alone. One of the more celebrated events of blockade-running on the Chattahoochee occurred in the spring of 1862 when the steamer *Jackson* managed to deliver ten thousand arms upriver to Eufaula. Apalachicola remained blockaded and subjected to periodic raids, however, throughout the war.[88]

Designs on an upriver attack by Union forces remained a potential threat throughout the war, however impractical—the river is so shallow in its lower reaches that no oceangoing vessel could ascend it, and even light-drafted steamers only at certain times of the year—but concern with such a venture nonetheless occupied considerable time and jangled many a nerve in the Eufaula area. For elaborate riverine defenses necessary to repel such an advance, local citizens looked to the state. In November 1862, the governors of Alabama, Georgia and Florida appealed to President Jefferson Davis to defend the Chattahoochee-Apalachicola-Flint river system. In response to concerns about the safety of the river's southern reaches, Davis organized the Middle Florida Military District, which included the Apalachicola River and its namesake city.[89]

Officials soon formulated plans to place obstructions in the river and construct a few strategic defensive positions as perhaps the most cost-effective deterrent to invasion of the region from the Gulf. Work on the plan proceeded haltingly, though, as securing labor for defensive measures along the river system proved to be a difficult task. Engineers, military authorities and local commissioners corresponded frequently on this problem. Few responded willingly to the many advertisements for "laborers," or hired slaves, that appeared throughout the region, such as the May 1862 appeal for "200 laborers," including "5 or 6 common carpenters, 1 or 2 ordinary bricklayers, and 4 good cooks."

After a less than enthusiastic response, Confederate officials began to make personal appeals to certain leading citizens and acquaintances in the area.

The State of Alabama,

To *Osborn Rogers* ....Dr.

To labor of....*2*....slaves from....*Dec, 24*....*1863*....to....*Jany 30. 1863,*....*66 days*

on Public Defenses on the Chattahoochee River—impressed by Wm. Abney, Agent, &c. at $.*1*....each per day, $.*66.00*..

I certify that the above account is correct.

Wm Abney

Impressing Agent for Barbour County.

Eufaula, *March 7th*....1863.

[*Examined & approved Eas S Shorter*]
[*Cmd dt Camp*]

Received of Wm. Abney, Impressing Agent for Barbour County, *Sixty six*....Dollars, in full of the above account.

March 7th....1863.

O Y Rogers
Par J M Spurlock

Receipt given to a local slaveholder for impressment of his slaves sent to work on Chattahoochee River defenses. *Eufaula Athenaeum.*

A Confederate engineer wrote to John McNab and William Thornton of Eufaula, for example, in May 1862 personally reminding them that he would "be obliged to you for your assistance in obtaining them. The Confederacy will pay, feed, and furnish the medical attendance and medicines, also shelter for these hands. It will be my special care to see that they are properly cared for so long as they are under my control." Exasperated, other agents at length sought permission to offer higher wages as an inducement. One frustrated agent recorded that it was "almost impossible to get hands from Columbus or Eufaula" but thought that a generous "$1 per day, medical attendance, rations, &c." might encourage better response. He attempted to send a telegraph to Eufaula to see what reaction there might be to such a plan, but an answer has not been recorded. The agent's efforts appear to not have been met with success, as shortly afterward, the mayor of Columbus visited Eufaula to confer with locals about cooperating to find laborers to prepare defenses on the river. At length realizing the hopelessness of the situation, they decided to wait until the crops were gathered in the fall to attempt to secure the laborers again. Conditions never improved, though, and as the war continued to overwhelm Confederate resources throughout the South, fortifying the Chattahoochee became less and less of a priority. Little significant engineering, outside the placement of a few batteries and obstructions on the Apalachicola, was ever done along the lower river.[90]

Eufaula did nonetheless become an unlikely center for Confederate navy activities. The Confederate Naval Iron Works complex upriver in Columbus, responsible for the construction of the CSS *Jackson*, the CSS *Chattahoochee* and numerous engines used in vessels across the Confederacy, maintained a subsidiary facility in Eufaula for most of the war. The enterprise began in the late 1850s as the Eufaula Iron Works, which advertised that it could furnish its customers with a wide variety to iron goods including sugar mills, gin gearing and fencing. Crucially to its future success, the operators noted in an 1860 advertisement that "[a]s everyone is using steam, we are prepared to give advice and build to order. Drawings for machinery free of charge where we build the Machinery. Particular attention given to repairing."

The Eufaula Iron Works morphed into two separate businesses in the summer of 1861, as cofounders James W. (Will) Young and W.G.A. Blair dissolved the partnership and went their separate ways. Young moved on to his new Steam Engine and Saw Mill Works, while Blair continued on with the Eufaula Iron and Brass Foundry. Apparently, Blair's outfit essentially took over the original business facility near the entrance to the road leading to the steamboat landing, while Young opened up a new shop nearby.

EUFAULA
IRON WORKS.

NOW is the time to send in your orders for Sugar Mills, Mill Gearing, Gin Gear, Gudgeons, Plates and Balls, Ploughs, Sash Weights, Spindles, Railing, Fencing. Veranda Columns, House, and Mill Iron generally.

The Eufaula Iron Works

are now prepared to furnish any of the above articles with neatness and dispatch. We will furnish STEAM ENGINES from one to thirty horse power, boilers and all complete, for

Mills, Gins, Presses, &c.

As every one is using steam, we are are prepared to give advice and build to order. Drawings for Machinery free of charge where we build the Machinery.

Particular attention given to repairing.

All orders sent by mail or otherwise, will be done as well as if the parties were present.

Terms CASH or City acceptance.

Blacksmithing, in all its branches, done on short notice.   JAMES W. YOUNG & CO.
                    Near the Steamboat Landing.

, All work delivered to Drays or Steamboats is at the risk of the owner.

Eufaula, Sept. 20th, 1859   26—1y

Eufaula Iron Works advertisement that appeared in the *Spirit of the South*. *Alabama Department of Archives and History.*

Young listed himself as the engineer and machinist for the Steam Engine and Saw Mill Works in early 1861, touting his ability to "build engines from 3 to 100 horse power, circular and upright saw mills, grist mills, steam gauges, whistles, oil cups and brass work generally," as well as the fact that he could fabricate to order "cylinder, flue, and tubular boilers" of the type used in steamboats.[91]

Young's facility primarily helped fit out vessels, procure equipment and construct steam machinery parts. By the spring of 1863, a crew of about a dozen machinists and blacksmiths was listed on the Eufaula facility's payroll, which continued in its work for the duration of the war. Young's involvement with the Confederate government apparently began through a business relationship with Naval Iron Works chief engineer John L. Warner. The son of Edward Young, it is likely that Will came to the attention of Warner through his father's connections. It is unknown when Will turned his business's attention toward the ironworks, but when he received notice of his being drafted into the Confederate army in September 1862, Warner wrote to the commanding conscription officer that Will's services "are required to work on machinery of Iron Clad Gun Boats. Mr. Young is the proprietor of a machine shop in Eufaula which I wish to start on this work in connection with these Works. I therefore respectfully request his detail for work under my supervision." Warner's appeal worked, and Will soon obtained the requested exemption.[92]

Young's Eufaula subsidiary facility produced several pieces of machinery used in construction of the *Jackson* and the *Chattahoochee* in Columbus. These parts and assorted other materials were ferried to and from Eufaula for various stages of manufacturing aboard steamboats. The steamer *Indian* seems to have been especially well used by the Naval Iron Works, as several times it delivered cargoes of steam pumps and tons of castings for Young's machine shop. The ironworks' ledger lists several shipments to Eufaula of white and red lead and special metal alloys that the Eufaula workmen converted from patterns into valves, piston heads and a variety of other parts. A hint of the skilled nature of the type of work Young's employees engaged in is revealed in some correspondence from Chief Engineer Warner to Young in 1864 in which he sent down a pattern for slide valves from Columbus and requested a drawing for a certain type of piston head in return.

At times, workers from each facility spent time in both cities as work on aspects of certain projects progressed. At least one officer of one of the boats constructed in Columbus, Lieutenant J.J. Guthrie, spent so much time in Eufaula that he bought a house there where his family lived during the war. In 1864, several officers of the *Chattahoochee* were living in Eufaula. In the closing months of the war, when Columbus at last came into the crosshairs of Union forces, Warner sent a number of valuable supplies used in ongoing projects for safekeeping in Eufaula. Among these were a variety of metals vital to the war effort but so increasingly scarce that they could not be replaced if lost, such as copper and sheet iron.[93]

The city of Eufaula actually figured into a plan to make use of the boats it helped construct to break the Union blockade at Apalachicola. The ambitious expedition called for an expeditionary force to capture a small blockading vessel and then for it to be used in turn to capture another ship patrolling just off Apalachicola. The gunboat *Chattahoochee*, already once sunk but repaired, headed out from Columbus for Eufaula on April 20, 1864, to transport many of the men involved in the scheme on the first leg of their journey. It took an astonishing two weeks for the beleaguered boat to travel to the Bluff City, where it finally arrived at the landing on May 3 after having been delayed twice by grounding. There it was to wait until a rise in the river could facilitate travel farther south. Meanwhile, the men of the expeditionary force continued on toward the Gulf on the steamer *Marianna*. They were later joined by a small group of volunteers in Florida and eventually transferred onto several smaller boats for the final approach to Apalachicola. To their frustration, shortly after arrival there, the men found that their plan had been discovered by the blockading force. Enemy preparedness, bad weather and a shortage of supplies compelled the men to abandon the effort as a complete failure. They decided to head back upriver, with the majority of the force making a narrow escape.[94]

Despite Eufaulians' focus on the river as an invasion route for Yankees, they actually had much more to fear from a marching army. With a small number of Confederate forces scattered throughout the region, Union leaders had contemplated a raid on the area, specifically targeting the large industrial complex at Columbus, as early as July 1864. On July 4, Brigadier General Alexander Asboth had proposed a strike into the lower Chattahoochee Valley, to be executed by two thousand "well mounted and armed" men to capture the storehouse region and its precious resources that might otherwise be brought to bear against Union armies in the field in Virginia and Georgia. His plans specifically mentioned Eufaula, calling for the destruction of the strategic telegraph lines in the city and the nearby railroad. Asboth's superiors, preoccupied with Lee's army in Virginia and the Confederate army defending Atlanta, did not act on the request.[95]

Army action elsewhere had a dramatic effect on life in Eufaula all the same. Due to its strategic location near river and rail transportation routes and its relative isolation from most of the fighting, Eufaula became a significant hospital center for Confederate forces. Hospitals as we know them did not exist in most parts of the South during the war, and the communities located near battles that resulted in thousands of casualties were totally unprepared to treat the wounded. Consequently, wounded were sent to area private homes, often a great distance away from the battlefield, to be nursed back to health by volunteers. As early as 1862, wounded Confederate soldiers from battles in the war's western theater were being sent to the city to recover from injuries received in combat. As the fighting grew to involve larger and larger armies closer to home, Eufaula's role as a hospital center increased. The fighting around Atlanta in the spring and summer of 1864 spurred a dramatic increase in medical activity in the city. The exact number of wounded in town at any given time is unknown, but it is likely that there were no more than a few dozen convalescing soldiers in area homes on any given day prior to the Atlanta Campaign. By the summer of 1864, when fighting in northern Georgia was at its height, however, the city was inundated with hundreds more wounded troops than it could effectively handle.[96]

Locals pressed several buildings into service as temporary hospitals to meet the crisis. The process by which this happened appears to have been anything but orderly and prescribed, as hotels, taverns and even the courthouse were all used as hospital facilities. The upper floors of many private homes throughout town, such as Fendall Hall, were converted into makeshift hospitals as well, while some families agreed to take in some of the less severe patients to make room for the more seriously wounded in the other "official" hospital facilities. After all volunteered structures had been filled, authorities resorted to the impressment of others. Even this step proved insufficient to deal with the influx of wounded that arrived from the reciprocal bludgeoning of General William T. Sherman's and General John B. Hood's armies in north Georgia, though. There was at least one building constructed specifically for the purpose of serving as a hospital, known as the "Bell Hospital," but the overflow of wounded troops became such that temporary sheds were built south of Broad Street to accommodate some of the men.[97]

Numerous local citizens, mostly women, helped staff and supply these hospitals to the degree they could, nursing men with bodies shattered by bullets and shrapnel, writhing in agony from the trauma of amputated arms or legs or suffering quietly from raging infection. Conditions were abysmal. Surgeon Paul D. Baker, who spent much of the war in Eufaula assisting the soldiers sent there for recovery, wrote in July 1864 that "between 200 and 300 wounded men" who had not eaten for several days arrived in town at one time. Despairing of his situation, Baker wrote despondently that he had absolutely no place for these men and had to lay them on the floors of houses whose occupants allowed for the use of the space. He had "no pans, no tubs, no spittoons, no medicines, no nurses, no ward masters, no adequate medical assistance, no hospital clothing, and consequently, cannot have the clothing of these men washed without turning them naked in the houses or in the streets."

Many locals went to work manufacturing a wide variety of necessary supplies that they could provide, especially lint bandages, and canvassed the community to procure food—a herculean task during the depressed wartime economic conditions. Despite all their effort, the Eufaula hospitals remained unpleasant and undersupplied throughout the height of their operations in the summer and fall of 1864. They brought the war home to Eufaulians as few other things could have, reminding them graphically of what the war could do to men. How many wounded soldiers died in the city is unknown, but their sufferings and the efforts of the community to care for them are an especially visceral part of the city's wartime narrative.[98]

Wounded Confederates were not the only sojourners from the front lines who spent time in Eufaula during the war. The city hosted a branch of Camp Sumter prison at Andersonville, Georgia, the infamous Confederate detention facility at which nearly 13,000 of approximately 45,000 Union prisoners died in the course of just over a year. The overcrowded prison quickly overwhelmed the resources of Confederate authorities and of the small town that hosted it during the summer and fall of 1864. To relieve the situation, early in 1865, officials at the prison determined to send some of the prisoners to a few other locations in the region. General John Imboden, a cavalry commander who, after narrowly surviving typhoid fever, had been assigned to command of prisoner of war camps in Georgia, advocated that only one satellite facility, Eufaula, be selected for "economical reasons." He advised it was "easier to supply two posts than four or five so widely scattered." Ultimately, however, between 500 and 1500 prisoners were kept at multiple small facilities scattered around Alabama, Georgia and South Carolina. Perhaps a few hundred were kept in Eufaula in the chaotic closing months of the war; available records are unclear. Imboden, coming to the conclusion that feeding these prisoners was at least as much of a problem as having them fight in the ranks against them, attempted to have them unconditionally paroled in Florida but was refused. They, along with wounded adversaries, distraught citizens and anxious slaves, would spend the last weeks of the war nervously waiting for the inevitable end to the conflict. Before the final curtain closed on the national drama, Eufaula itself would come into the crosshairs of Union forces.[99]

Chapter 6
"Fear Was Depicted on Every Face"

The Federal troops who finally ventured to the environs of Eufaula converged on the area from extreme north and south Alabama, respectively. Major General Benjamin H. Grierson, in command of about four thousand troopers, left Blakeley, located on Mobile Bay opposite of the city of Mobile, on April 17, 1865. He had designs on destroying remaining Confederate supply depots and assisting General James H. Wilson's cavalry force that was then sweeping south from north Alabama targeting the industrial centers of Selma and Columbus. With Lee's army already surrendered, the campaigns would be among the last of the war and would ensure that Eufaula, which had been so prominent in initiating secession, would be in the headlines as the war ended.[100]

The first concern of those in Eufaula in April 1865 lay with Wilson, whose advance had been followed with trepidation since he had crossed the rain-swollen Tennessee River in late March. Fear based on rumor turned into mortal terror in Eufaula upon receipt of the news that Wilson's cavalry, conducting a lightning-like raid through the heart of what remained of the Confederacy, had sacked Selma and captured Montgomery and now had Columbus in its sights. Many feared that Eufaula's time had come, and it would soon be put to the torch. In a rehearsal for the actual arrival of Union troops in the town later, the city and its environs briefly became a sort of confused crossroads, as the trains and roads suddenly filled with people coming and going in various degrees of confusion. In the bustle, refugees seeking to stay ahead of the Union advance crossed paths with volunteers

Major General Benjamin H. Grierson, who commanded the cavalry force that captured Eufaula in 1865. *Library of Congress.*

headed north to fight the invaders. Wilson's focus remained on the Confederate industrial complex upriver, though, and his troopers came no closer than fifty miles of Eufaula. Instead, it would be Grierson's smaller force advancing from the southwest that would ultimately target the city.[101]

Grierson heard of Wilson's capture of Columbus in Greeneville, Alabama. He immediately adapted his plans in an effort to coordinate with him on the capture of Macon and Augusta, Georgia, dividing his force into two columns. One he sent toward Union Springs, and with the other he set his sights squarely on Eufaula. Grierson reached Troy, Alabama, on April 26. Near there, he first heard rumors of the armistice between the forces under the command of General Joseph T. Johnston and General William T. Sherman. Realizing that Johnston's army was the only sizable Confederate force left in the field and that this might mean the war was effectively over, he immediately issued orders prohibiting his men from foraging except for necessary sustenance for them and their horses. Upon reaching the Pea River, his army crossed into Barbour County over Hobdy's Bridge, made forever famous in local lore as the location of a bloody battle in the late Second Creek War a generation earlier. The Union troopers passed through the community of Louisville and encamped at Bethlehem Church near Clayton on their advance toward the Chattahoochee.

Along the way, Grierson's men exchanged their by now worn-out horses and mules for fresh mounts by appropriating those of farmers and plantation owners whose property they came near. It seemed the beginning of the type of raid locals had long feared, and word of the cavalry's advance spread like wildfire throughout Barbour County. A slave became the first to alert the town of Clayton to the Union force's approach, having been sent off hurriedly by a local planter. Neither slave nor freemen knew exactly what to expect at the hands of the invaders. As it turned out, neither did Grierson know exactly what to expect of those whose homes he had invaded.[102]

Grierson admitted in his memoirs that he did not expect to meet much resistance along his route, but he "realized the fact that we were passing through a region that had been in the undisturbed possession of the rebels for several years" and consequently advanced carefully. The war might be rapidly coming to a close, but that did not mean that the people of southeast Alabama would necessarily allow the first Union cavalry most of them had seen to pass unmolested. He was relieved to see, though, that he was greeted periodically by small delegations of worried local citizens who were "quick to perceive their true situation of affairs and capable of appreciating our lenience and courtesy." These people he sent back to their homes to let their neighbors know that the Union troopers were indeed not bent on the destruction of their communities.[103]

Victoria Clayton remembered that it was about noon on April 28, 1865, when she first caught sight of the "glittering bayonets" of the approaching blue-clad column in the distance along the Louisville road as she stood watching from her home. Filing past her view, Grierson's men leisurely entered Clayton minutes later. The small town, founded in the 1830s, served as county seat and was home to some of most vocal secessionists in state. While it posed no threat and was of little value to the Federals, citizens had very real reason to fear for its safety. Who could say for sure just how far the words of men like Jefferson Buford had traveled? Fully understanding that the gig was finally up, wealthy locals chose accommodation instead of arms with which to welcome their uninvited guests.

Benjamin Petty, a local merchant, quickly stepped forward to offer Grierson his home, the Octagon House, as a temporary headquarters office. Hailing from New York, Petty had been suspected by some as harboring Unionist sympathies anyway. His home, based on a unique approach to domestic architecture that became popular in the 1850s primarily in the Northeast, was one of only a handful of its type in Alabama. Fellow townspeople soon joined Petty in his hospitality, as the nearby Miller-Martin Town House served as host for a hastily arranged dinner party held for Union officers on the evening of their arrival. Grierson returned the show of good faith. Having been notified by a concerned acquaintance of the potential danger to Mrs. Clayton's home, as she was the wife of a prominent Confederate officer, he posted a guard at the property's entrance to ensure that no troopers would be able to inflict any untoward retribution. Already, Confederate soldiers in the area on leave, official or otherwise, were coming to him to surrender and be paroled.[104]

Not everyone in Clayton greeted Grierson cordially. As a group of three Federal troopers canvassed the outskirts of town looking for mules that could be appropriated for their use, an unidentified sniper or snipers hidden in the woods fired on the bluecoats. One of the shots struck and killed Private Joseph C. Marlin of Company K, Second New Jersey Cavalry. "What a waste, I thought, of a good man," wrote fellow cavalryman Townsend Walmsley. "We all knew Joe, and now he would not be going home with us to his home and family. Yes, even a soldier can shed a tear, if he is alone." The man was buried where he had fallen. As Marlin was a veteran of the cavalry's many campaigns, his fate proved to be especially tragic. The next day, word of Confederate surrender became general in the ranks.[105]

As the troops moved out of Clayton on the twenty-ninth, headed for Eufaula, word of the cessation of hostilities spread in the ranks, lifting spirits. A short time later, though, they also learned of Lincoln's assassination. Grierson noted that he was at first "filled with amazement" but thought the awful rumor "really too horrible to be true." Upon confirmation that "the heinous crime had been perpetrated," he did his best to restrain his emotional troops, whom he feared might at any moment lay to ashes the communities through which they were passing out of a sense of rightful revenge. According to one of the troopers, the assassination caused a shock in the ranks more electric than the surrender. In his diary, Townsend Walmsley recorded bluntly that "now our feelings were shot down to hell." He also remembered that he "felt the lump in my throat, crowding, the rest of the day." He noted that "a state of quietude spread throughout our entire Brigade like a soft shock-wave. This Hush enveloped everyone the entire day and around our evening campfires. Finally when taps was sounded, it was barely audible."[106]

Even had they known the troopers' sober state of mind, the people of Eufaula and its immediate environs would have found it difficult to be any more frightened. Couriers went from house to house in the area, frantically warning residents of the approach of the Yankees. "The explosion of a bomb in each one's yard could not have created greater excitement," recorded Parthenia Hague. Having been reading for years about the destruction in war-torn Virginia, neighboring Georgia and a host of other places in the South that had been subject to Federal raids, residents trembled for the city's fate. "What a fearful day it was for us," remembered Hague, "when in April, 1865 word came into our placid valley that the Northern army was almost at our doors! I could not begin to describe our chagrin and terror…Fear was depicted on every face, for who could tell but that the morrow's sun would cast its beams upon a heap of smoking ruins, and we be bereft of all the property we had."

All normal activities, such as what existed in a city that was entering its fifth wartime spring, ceased as citizens decided how or if they should meet the impending crisis. Schools closed, plantation owners stopped work and what little business activity there was came to a halt. Swirling rumors as to exactly when the horsemen would appear in town only added to the anxiety. Some breathlessly asserted that they were only a mile away and would enter the city in mere minutes, while others swore that they heard gunfire or saw telltale smoke on the horizon. Horses tramping over a bridge startled the residents of an outlying community, whose hearts froze with the surety that the Yankees were upon them. "In painful apprehension we sat long on the porch," recorded Parthenia Hague. "God only knows how fervent and plaintive was the prayer that ascended that April night in southern Alabama, from hundreds of dwellings peopled only by women, children, and negro slaves."[107]

Slaves indeed lifted prayers to heaven as the raiders approached, but they may not have been requesting the same sort of salvation as their white brothers and sisters. A vague sense that the arrival of the Federal force might lead to permanent freedom prevailed among the slave community, but after generations of being abused by white men, they were naturally cautious about the intentions of the armed invaders about whom they had heard so many negative comments. Who could say but that the plight of the slave might somehow be made worse, or that they would merely be exchanging one set of masters for another?

Many slaves, as did their masters, simply tried to hide until they knew what the arrival of the armed contingent might mean for them. Former slave Maugan Shepherd remembered years later that he and many other slaves were so "powerful scared of de Yankee soldiers" when they came through the town that their only recourse was to conceal themselves in hopes that the troopers would not tarry long in the city. Elsewhere, slaves at one plantation who had heard Yankees had arrived in the area gathered at their master's house to see if they could catch a glimpse of the troops. "Perhaps some may have come with the design of going with the Yankees," indignantly observed a witness. One slave sarcastically remarked years later that her master had been even more afraid of the Yankees than the slave population, as he hid "unceremoniously" in the woods upon their approach and did not emerge from his concealment for nearly a week.[108]

Word of Grierson's approach sparked a mad scramble to hide from the invaders valuables such as silver, furniture, wine and a variety of precious

Maugan Shepherd. *Library of Congress.*

foodstuffs. Numerous residents of the area, both white and black, were to be found engaged in this pursuit in the hours before the troops arrived. They resorted to all measure of means to accomplish their task. Parthenia Hague recalled that "it was amusing, as well as sad, to see a feather-bed protruding at least a quarter of its length from a carriage window" as residents attempted to evacuate before the Union force. "In our great anxiety, appearances were not regarded. The single thought of the people was to protect themselves and their property as expeditiously and securely as possible." Even livestock herds were turned from the fields into the roads to get away from the oncoming Federal fury that seemed to be upon them. One woman wrapped all her jewelry in an old rag and tossed it into a rosebush in her front yard. Yankee troops ransacked the house, opening bureau drawers and turning over beds, but the treasure in plain view escaped their notice. One family wrapped a quantity of bacon in cloth and put it in the ash hopper for safekeeping. An enterprising young lady wore three dresses in layers in the hope that the Yankees might not destroy them, while one resident of Eufaula hid sugar, hams, other groceries and silverware in a narrow space between the ceiling and roof of her house. Another person placed some items in a jar and lowered the contents into a well with the water bucket, while one farmer reportedly placed a small collection of valuables under a nesting hen. Other residents, thinking ahead and getting an earlier start to the regional game of hide-and-seek, conceived of even more elaborate plans. One person, at the suggestion of a trusted slave, dug a large hole in the family vegetable garden wherein was placed its supply of sugar, syrup, wine and other items. Cabbage was planted on top of the hoard, which had started to grow by the time the soldiers passed.[109]

Not everyone was so lucky. The troops did take possession of provisions—a term broadly defined by them, to be sure—as they determined they needed along their route. "I knew families that were bereft of everything," indignantly remembered Hague. She claimed to have seen households after the raid "who had not so much left as would furnish one meal of victuals… In many instances women and children would have to stand by helpless, and see their trunks, bureaus, and wardrobes kicked open. Whatever struck the soldier's fancy was appropriated." Others simply found themselves at the wrong place at the wrong time.

One unlucky family attempting to escape from Union advances on the city of Mobile for the supposed safety of Eufaula happened to run literally right into the Federal column in the roads outside of town. The cavalrymen cut their horses from the reins. "The wife begged to be spared the horses, but finding pleading to no avail, she let loose her tongue in such a way that one of the soldiers raised his gun and threatened to shoot her if she did not keep quiet. She stood fair and fearless, and told him to shoot." Hague noted that the trooper "was not so heartless, however, as to put his threat into execution." The road from Clayton to Eufaula, however, was not marked with the desolation that characterized Sherman's route across Georgia. Available evidence indicates that relatively few incidents involving serious destruction of property occurred, and instead the cavalry's arrival can be characterized more by theft of all manner of livestock and property than outright destruction.[110]

Confirmation of the proximity of the Federals reached Eufaula on the afternoon of April 28, 1865. There were no Confederate troops in town capable of mounting even token resistance. Even the Home Reserves had decided to disband in the realization that any resistance they could muster would be futile and very likely counterproductive. Local leaders—including the city's provost marshal, Captain A.F. Pagnier, and presumably the mayor—hastily met and decided to meet the emergency head-on; they would send out a delegation to meet Grierson on the road into town under a flag of truce, hoping they might dissuade him from setting the city to the torch once informed of the surrender Lee's army and the seemingly inevitable surrender of Johnston's, of which they had heard rumors but could not as yet confirm. As far as they were concerned, the war was over. Edward Young's teenage son, Ed, and another young man named Edward Stern mounted horses and, bearing white flags, set out to perform the solemn duty. To their surprise, they did not see any Federal force even though they traveled several miles out of town. No doubt bewildered at their unceremonious return, local leaders immediately sent the riders back out, convinced that the Federal column was just a short distance away. Some back in town may have briefly wondered if Grierson had for some unknown reason decided to skirt the town altogether.[111]

The young men set out again, this time staying overnight at the home of a Mr. Cunningham, who lived along the Clayton Road. They caught sight of the Union cavalry's advance guard along the Batesville Road at about dawn on April 29, 1865. Near a creek a few miles out of town known locally as "Six Mile Branch," they encountered Grierson himself. There, in the crowd of the commander's escort on a quiet, dusty road through the wilderness, they delivered the message that there would be no military resistance awaiting the Federals in Eufaula. Their exact words are lost to history, but it is clear that they hoped to persuade the city's soon-to-be captors to conduct a peaceful occupation. Their mission accomplished, they turned their horses toward Eufaula and galloped off.

When they arrived back in town, Mayor C.J Pope and a number of other local officials had gathered to greet them and hear of their conference. Not knowing for certain Grierson's intentions, they desired to put words to action and provide the warmest welcome they could in the hopes of saving the imperiled city from the whims of the invading force. The mayor himself, along with James L. Pugh and several members of the city council, rode out to meet Grierson just west of College Hill and escort him into Eufaula. Atop the hill, with the spires of the town's churches and the roofs of its struggling businesses in view, they met the Union commander and his officer staff. Grierson remembered the scene as "presenting remarkably picturesque scenery that might well fill with emotion the heart of an artist."[112]

After an exchange of pleasantries between nervous local dignitaries and the Union officers, the column entered town along what was then called the Clayton Road with a band playing "Yankee Doodle." Stretched out as they were along the road quite some distance, even as the column had been "closed up," the passage took several hours. Descending College Hill, they passed stately residences and a number of more modest homes, most of which were shuttered or had curtains drawn out of a combination of terror and disgust. Grierson recalled that it seemed as if "the people must have departed to some other region, or suddenly died, so quietly were they housed within doors." Some, though, were surely watching secretly, taking in the spectacle of an invading army. At least one local citizen made no efforts to hide his feelings about the invaders. Professor J.C. Van Houten, a blind musician who instructed young ladies in the arts of music at Union Female College, boldly responded to the Northern musicians' celebratory anthem. Sitting on the porch of a house on Broad Street, he picked up his violin and defiantly bowed "Dixie" as the troops passed by. Later asked what sparked his actions, he simply said that the instrument refused to play any other tune that day.[113]

If the Federals were offended by the musician's bravado, they made no display of their displeasure. The column made an orderly entry into town, which Grierson put under military rule upon arrival. The general chose to disturb life in Eufaula as little as possible, and by all reports, his men went about their daily routines after only the briefest of interruptions. Perhaps at the behest of locals, he even ordered his command to march over the covered bridge spanning the Chattahoochee and set up camp in the broad expanse of riverside fields bordering the community of Georgetown, Georgia. There they were to await further orders while he determined his next moves. Grierson's staff meanwhile moved into temporary headquarters at the Howard Hotel in Eufaula, where the Federal commander finally sat down to put together a report on his activities along his march from Mobile to send to his superiors. By the time he forwarded the telegram, he had already received confirmation of the armistice between Sherman and Johnston from other Union leaders in the region. He immediately ordered all the Confederate soldiers he had captured en route to Eufaula paroled and began sorting out what needed to be done next.[114]

The unexpected effort to turn Eufaula into a Confederate state capital immediately prior to Grierson's arrival may have caused him to question the calm acceptance of inevitable defeat to which many in the town seemed to have been resigned. Earlier in April, the bulk of the state archives of Alabama had been shipped via two six-mule wagon teams to Eufaula from Montgomery once it became clear that Alabama's capital city lay in the path of Wilson's raiders. One can only imagine the astonishment with which disheartened locals would have greeted the cargo and state agent John B. Taylor, whose arrival was damning testimony of the impotence of Confederate arms to resist the invaders any longer. But the agent was to be just the precursor of a wholesale emergency move of the operations of the Alabama state government. Before the transfer could be affected, however, the war had ended.[115]

Most of the details of the mechanics of the last-ditch effort to move the state capital have been lost to history, as is the case with so much in the frenetic last days of the Confederacy. Besides the fact that Governor Thomas Hill Watts and other key officials had decided to flee Montgomery as Wilson's men approached, we have little knowledge of exactly what plans were made for the establishment of Eufaula as the seat of state government. Perhaps, in the chaos of the collapse, no concrete plans had been made at all, and suitable quarters for housing government activities were to be identified upon the arrival of officials. There is no information that any of these men ever made it to the Bluff City; Governor Watts himself was arrested near Union Springs on May 1, by which time word of the capture of Eufaula would have certainly been general in the area. The aborted attempt to administer Alabama's government functions from Eufaula unceremoniously ended the city's era as a Confederate municipality. Among the first to advocate for secession, it had become among the last places in Alabama to fall to Union occupation. With the Confederacy defeated and state and local civil authorities barely functioning, Eufaulians braced themselves for a peace that threatened to be every bit as volatile as war had been.[116]

Chapter 7

"To Restore Order Out of Such Chaos"

Eufaula's transition to peace began with a martial proclamation. Grierson's first move in his occupation of the city was to issue orders for the maintenance of order during his stay. In General Orders No. 6, issued on May 1, 1865, he set forth the ground rules that would be followed while his troops were in town. The communiqué listed five rules that would guide the interaction between the soldiers and the townspeople:

First. The soldiers of this command are forbidden to interfere with the persons or property of citizens.

Second. During the existing armistice Confederate officers and soldiers will be permitted to pass to their home unmolested.

Third. Citizens will continue their legitimate business, but will not be allowed to congregate upon the streets.

Fourth. The patrol heretofore organized by the civil authorities will confine themselves to the government of citizens and Confederate soldiers, and will not interfere with the U.S. forces.

Fifth. Captain E.E. Thornton is announced as provost-marshal, and a sufficient provost guard has been organized to insure quiet and order.[117]

The rules were generous, essentially allowing the city to preserve its autonomy and officially forbidding the type of plundering of private property that residents had so long feared. It was as much of a fast track to normalcy as the victorious invaders could reasonably offer given the circumstances. With the city secured, Grierson began notifying other Union forces in the area of the cessation of hostilities and instructed them to link up with him by moving by "easy stages toward Montgomery." Union units were instructed to "only take from the inhabitants what is necessary to subsist your command."[118]

The Yankees did not allow everything in Eufaula to go untouched, however. They quickly targeted for destruction the contents of the local Confederate commissary, located on Randolph Street in the middle of the block stretching from Broad to Barbour Streets. A large supply of whiskey, reputedly kept to distribute to the many wounded and sick Confederate soldiers still recuperating in Eufaula, became the special target of the raiders. The Union troopers broke into the facility soon after arrival and made short work of the disposal of the spirits by pouring barrels of alcohol into the street. The flow sparked a comical assemblage of men and beasts that created an atmosphere of farce for the dissolution of the Confederate war effort and embarrassed many upstanding citizens. Mary Barnett later remembered that she saw men, "both black and white," on their hands and knees lapping up the whiskey alongside a number of hogs that had been allowed to roam unattended. She noted that soon after, many of both ingloriously staggered drunkenly in the streets before falling over and passing out. Grierson ordered his men to distribute the wide variety of other supplies found in the commissary to the city's poor, of which there were many.[119]

How to handle the hundreds of boxes of state records that they found had recently been shipped to the city proved to be a little more complicated task. Simply identifying whom they all belonged to challenged the Federals. While most of the assorted records clearly were the property of the State of Alabama, mixed in with them, somehow, were a quantity of papers from the State of Mississippi and a number of materials belonging to the Missouri legislature. Agent Taylor, the man entrusted with the records for safekeeping upon the evacuation of Montgomery, asked for the assistance of Federal troops in returning the records to Montgomery. Twelve six-mule wagons transported the bulk of the state archives from Eufaula to the capital city in late May, while another 175 boxes of papers were sent upriver to Columbus aboard the steamboat *Indian* and then overland via railroad.

The saga of the state archives dragged on for some time. In November 1865, officials discovered that a small portion of the records, which had been placed in a local storehouse, had been overlooked in preparing the original shipments. Upon the request of the secretary for Alabama's provisional governor, Lewis Parsons, they were belatedly sent back. As would be expected, an undetermined number of state records were lost in all these transfers. While most of the bound books, including a large number of journals and ledgers, apparently survived their journeys, the same cannot be said of the immense quantity of loose papers with which they were transported.[120]

However, the victorious Union military tracked more closely one particular bit of Confederate property that appeared in Eufaula. Sometime shortly after Grierson's capture of the town, a curious little torpedo boat, built as a special covert project by the Confederate Naval Iron Works upriver, drifted past the bluff, towed behind a steamboat bound for Apalachicola. Designed as a blockade-buster, the low-lying *Viper,* operated by a small crew of perhaps six or eight, had been designed to do its work in tandem with a larger "mother ship" such as the ironclad *Jackson.* It is believed to have featured a spar at the end of which could be placed a "torpedo" mine designed to explode against the hull of an enemy ship upon impact or perhaps even be detonated remotely by means of a cable.

Abandoned to the Yankee captors of Columbus a short distance downriver from its launching point, it became an object of no little attention. Apparently owing to the ingenuity in its design, it managed to be preserved while everything else in the way of war materiel the bluecoats burned, smashed, sunk or confiscated. Intrigued with its construction, they had it towed to the Gulf, where it could be taken further to a naval base in Key West. Its planned journey came to an abrupt halt on May 25 in a storm near Tampa, when it sunk in sixty fathoms of water and took its secrets, the "very forefront of naval technology" of the day, down to the bottom of the sea. It is interesting to speculate that it may have contained some of the most sophisticated engineering performed by Will Young's Eufaula foundrymen; it almost certainly contained some of their handiwork. Regardless of any local role in the unique craft's construction, it no doubt caused a stir in a port city that had never seen something quite like it.[121]

Grierson and his men did not spend the bulk of their time in Eufaula transporting records or towing torpedo boats. Grierson himself, by all accounts, rather made himself at home during his brief stay in the city, and several prominent citizens called on him. Mayor Pope hosted him and his staff for a dinner at his home with several other dignitaries in attendance, and others in town did likewise. At one dinner, Grierson, a former music teacher, fondly recalled the surprising musical talent on display in the community and even played some music himself. The general seems to have been generally well regarded, so much so that one person who chronicled his visit remarked that he was a true "gentleman"—the ultimate compliment for a man of the day in the South—and returned graciously the respect offered him by the city. Not everyone extended him the deference he might have thought due, though. While being entertained at the home of John McNab, the host's young daughter entered the room. Grierson kneeled and asked for a kiss, but the little girl, perhaps manifesting four years of overheard expressions of hatred of Yankees, refused him the honor. Lewis Jones, the black man who had famously delivered on horseback the telegram alerting the town of Clayton and surrounding areas of the secession of South Carolina and Alabama four years earlier, reputedly introduced himself to Grierson and noted his feat with pride.[122]

Area slaves were generally not so bold as Jones with Grierson. While many slaves fully understood the arrival of the Union soldiers as the official declaration of their freedom, they greeted them from a distance as they neither fully trusted their would-be liberators might not abuse them nor that their new condition would be upheld. Former slave Gus Askew, who witnessed the entry of Grierson's men into Eufaula, summed up the circumspection with which many slaves viewed the cavalrymen in an interview in his later years. "Mr. Lincoln done said we was free," he reminisced, "but us lil' niggers was too skeered to lissen to any ban' music, even iffen the so'jers had come to set us free…us was allus gittin' in somebody's way in dem days." He went on to note that slaves he knew nevertheless rejoiced in the moment and the possibilities it held. They simply "went away from the so'jers and had a good time 'mongst ourselves like we always done when there wasn't any cotton pickin."

Other Eufaula-area slaves decided to take their chances and perhaps get a jump-start on life as freedmen by following Grierson's column when it moved out of town, searching for a combination of safety and opportunity. Many may not have ever returned to the area in which they had so long lived as bondsmen, bravely embarking on a new life elsewhere. A few, however, are reported to have come back to the only home they had known, dissatisfied with either being forced to work as laborers for the troopers or disillusioned at the prospects they perceived before them. At least one welcomed the bluecoats while simultaneously questioning their ability to lead them anywhere. Former slave Hannah Irwin recalled with amusement how one Yankee soldier asked her about all the "white flowers" he had seen on his march. "You'd think that a gentleman with all them decorations on hisself woulda knowed a field of cotton," she noted amusedly.[123]

While Grierson's men spent most of their time in camp across the Chattahoochee rather than interacting with locals, they did maintain a visible presence in Eufaula. Changing guards were stationed at certain points in the city, and soldiers routinely marched along Broad and Randolph Streets on the way to and from the former Confederate commissary, which was transformed to a base of supply for the victorious invaders. In fact, the facility became a key part of their operational infrastructure, supporting the posting of several small bodies of troops throughout southeastern Alabama and southwestern Georgia by serving as a hub for regional distribution of supplies. A sense of the scale of this temporary activity can be gathered by the fact that in a single shipment in June 1865, more than fifty thousand rations were delivered at one time.

The Federals occupied themselves as best they could during the spring and summer of 1865, and their stay proved relatively uneventful. On any given day, several could be seen from the bluff casually fishing in the river. Even if locals got used to seeing the troopers in their midst, their presence was never exactly welcome. Eufaula resident Mollie E. Young wrote to her fiancée, former army surgeon Hamilton M. Weedon, some two months after the capture of the city, complaining that "the Yankees are still here, but as they are not allowed to enter private houses without a special invitation we are not troubled with them, though they have been invited to two or three houses to dine and take tea…I wish they could feel it their duty to return home, as I am sure none of us would be very sad at their departure."[124]

Perhaps the highlight event of an otherwise uneventful occupation was something that ended up not involving Eufaula at all. With the collapse of the Confederacy, President Jefferson Davis and his cabinet became fugitives, first attempting to futilely carry on government on the run and then unceremoniously fleeing capture individually. Davis's escape route took him through southern Georgia. For all anyone knew, it might even have taken him to the Eufaula area. An all-out dragnet soon swung into motion in an effort to capture the leader of the Rebellion—and, simultaneously, the accolades of the victorious Northern states and a unique place in the annals of American history.

General Wilson, having moved on to Macon after sacking Columbus's industrial complex, sent out men in search of him—some of whom may have been disguised as Confederates—and authorized detachments of Federal units in the area to fan out along the region's roads and rivers to lay the trap. He ordered General R.H.G. Minty, who commanded a number of troops in the area, to send men to the regional transportation centers of Cuthbert,

Georgia, and Eufaula, hoping that if they did not capture him there, they would surely funnel him toward another blocked course of escape. Taking no chances, Wilson attempted to eliminate any hope of safe harbor Davis might have enjoyed among the local populace by having published hundreds of handbills alerting citizens to the generous financial reward for his capture offered by President Andrew Johnson. The suspense proved to be short-lived in the Eufaula area, as Federals ultimately captured Davis on May 10 at Irwinville, some 120 miles to the east in south-central Georgia. With the final flicker of light in the Confederate candle extinguished, there seemed to be a collective exhale of soldiers and civilians alike in Eufaula. It was time to begin the transition to peace.[125]

"For a few weeks, it seemed as though we were petrified, scarcely knowing which way to turn, to restore order out of such chaos," remembered Parthenia Hague. "Our cause was lost, all our homes more or less despoiled, the whole South seemingly almost hopelessly ruined," she lamented in memory of the literal void of authority in the area. Great uncertainty prevailed, as the future seemed full of as many questions as answers. Yes, the South had lost the war and the slaves were freed. But how would society adjust to these new realities? Indeed, whether it would adjust at all became a serious question. General Grierson included his frank assessment of the situation in a report on his operation, noting that "[t]he poor people, including the returned Confederate private soldiers, are, as a general thing, now loyal; but the far greater portion of the wealthy classes are still very bitter in their sentiments against the Government, and clutch on to slavery with a lingering hope to save at least a relic of their favorite yet barbarous institution for the future."

Within weeks, it became apparent to even the occupying Union troops that there would at least be an attempt at reunification, if for no other reason than the people were so sick of war. General James H. Wilson, putting into succinct words in a report to his superiors in Washington what many observers and residents seemed to be feeling, notified them that he had been told by "men of good judgment and unquestioned loyalty that seven-eighths of the people are ready and anxious for a return to their duties as citizens without slavery and under the laws of the land, whatever they may be." After four years of privation, bloodshed and sorrow, residents of the Eufaula area looked forward to a restoration of some degree of normality.[126]

Beginning the process was not easy. The Eufaula area in the summer of 1865 lay in the center of a downtrodden region. "Never was a country so demoralized as this is," a depressed John Horry Dent recorded. "Were it not for the Yankee troops in the country to keep down these wretches, anarchy would prevail." Land was worth one-tenth of its prewar price, supplies of any sort were difficult to obtain and the region was painfully short of horses and mules—the result of prolonged impressment by both Confederate and Union forces. Armed bands of desperate marauders roamed the area, and law enforcement of any type proved slow to recover from the disruption of war.

The most dramatic change, however, lay in the absence of the institution of slavery. Freedom for slaves did not occur all at once in the area. Some had emancipated themselves by fleeing their masters during the war, while others marked their first day as freedmen as the day of the Yankees' arrival. Still others, unsure of the best course of action, waited for owners to confirm their freedom personally. Henry D. Clayton, for example, promptly gathered his slaves upon his return from military service and told them that they were free and could choose for themselves whether to stay on as hired hands or take their chances elsewhere. With few options available at the moment, most stayed. Many former bondsmen in the area made similar choices, choosing the security of familiarity over uncertainty.

Several former slaves who decided to remain on plantations as wage earners did soon reconsider their decisions. John Horry Dent recorded in his journal that some of his former slaves who had at first agreed to stay on as his employees were still "running away" to the Yankees as freedmen in the summer of 1865. Some, finding no safety among the Union occupiers, who sometimes worked them even harder than had their former masters, came back. Dent noted with condescension and a small bit of satisfaction that one set of his former slaves returned in the late summer "looking ill and used up. They ask pardon and promise to do better, saying they had their fill of the Yankees." This hesitancy to flee and seeming willingness to stay with former masters in no way indicates that freedmen were apathetic about their new status or somehow preferred servitude to freedom; it simply reveals what few choices they really had in a society that might no longer legally classify them as slaves but had no intention of allowing them a true measure of freedom. The saga of their quest for equality is, in essence, the primary narrative connecting so many of the scattered threads of Southern history from Appomattox to Selma and thus is far beyond the scope of this book. Exactly what their fate would be was anybody's guess in the summer of 1865, but the freedmen of the Eufaula area faced the uncertainty with a boldness and courage every bit as remarkable as their endurance of the institution from which they had just been freed.[127]

As the freedmen began to come to terms with their place in a post-slavery society, so did the defeated warriors who began to straggle back home. For weeks after the surrender, weary Confederate veterans, individually and in groups, could be seen on the roads around Eufaula. One Union trooper who participated in Grierson's raid observed that "we could now see along the roadway, hundreds of paroled and discharged ex-Confederate soldiers, each going to their own destinations. Ragged, unshaven, thin and haggard, now anxious to get home. May our God bless them and their families. They are going to need the Almighty's help if they are to exist." "The return of our soldiers after the surrender," remembered Parthenia Hague, "in their worn and ragged gray, as they tramped home by twos, threes, and sometimes in little squads of half a dozen or more, was pitiable in the extreme…Some were entirely without shoes or hats; others had only an apology for shoes and hats. They were coming home with nothing; and we could almost say, coming home to nothing." As they entered Eufaula, many had to show paroles to Federal guards but were otherwise unmolested. The reunions must have been emotional and heartwarming, even if a few were at first greeted like strangers owing to the fact that the privations of military life had so changed their appearance that they were sometimes not immediately recognized even by close kin.[128]

The thing most noticeable about the homecoming was that so many fewer returned than had left. The war decimated the ranks of the young men who had gone off to fight; 50 percent casualty rates among units raised in the Eufaula area were not uncommon. Of the 140 who originally enrolled in the Barbour Light Artillery, for example, only 60 survived the war. Many of those who did manage to survive were scarred for life, either physically or emotionally. Battlefield wounds crippled many, and the ravages of persistent or prolonged illness scarred many more. William C. Oates, the young man who had run to the Eastern National Bank to cash a check at the onset of the war, returned without a right arm. Leonard Y. Dean lost one of his arms at the Battle of Seven Pines. At least two local men lost legs, John W. Tullis a foot and Judson Brannon part of a foot, and Charlie Hart was crippled "the rest of his life" from an unspecified wound. These are just the accounts that have survived in local histories. Others returned with faces and bodies smashed and deformed to various degrees by bullets—lingering and visible reminders of what they had experienced. Less visible but equally debilitating were the mental scars that changed personalities, inhibited normal social interaction and weighed heavily on the mind at all times and manifested themselves as a sort of chronic depression. Eufaulians of the era did not yet have a name for posttraumatic stress disorder, but they well knew its effects.[129]

There were at least a few people, such as John Ridley Buford, who simply would not or could not come to terms with Confederate defeat. Rather than

Leonard Y. Dean, who lost his arm in the Battle of Seven Pines, at the postwar marriage of his daughter, Carolyn Simpson Dean. *Rob Schaffeld.*

attempt to rebuild his life in the reconstructed Union, Ridley in 1867 moved to Santa Barbara, Brazil, to join a small colony of Southern refugees that was part of a large group of expatriates from Alabama, Georgia and Tennessee. There they lived as farmers, attempting to carry on the Southern traditions they grew up with as best they could, leaving one of the more unique legacies of the Civil War in an unlikely location in rural South America.[130]

Those of Eufaula's veterans who did stay became storytellers and celebrated local connections to a fabled larger-than-life past—residents loved to hear their tales of adventure and hardship told and retold. Locals never tired of hearing of their struggles in camps and prisons and the desperate fights in which they were engaged. In the parlors, dining rooms and stores of Eufaula, their deeds on battlefields at Bull Run, Vicksburg, Gettysburg and Atlanta were often recounted. Local resident John G. Archibald told his story to many and became especially well remembered. He reputedly carried the Fifteenth Alabama's colors in some of the thickest fights of the war and supposedly hid the bullet-riddled flag in his shirt at Appomattox so that it could be taken home as a treasured memento. Parthenia Hague remembered wistfully how those she knew "were always deeply interested in hearing them [the veterans] recount, when we met them at social gatherings at some neighbor's house, the straits to which they were reduced toward the last days of the war, and on the home march after the surrender."

Vicariously, city residents lived the war over again through the stories they heard, experiencing its tragedy in a new but profoundly personal way that was passed down to their children and beyond. As was the case all across the South, the stories of heroism on the battlefield experienced by a relative few proved a more glorious and enduring memory than the hardships experienced at home by the many. Perhaps the veneration of these heroes and the stories they told helped civilians make sense of the chaos that had wrecked so many families and disrupted the lives of everyone so that the cause became, on some level, worthy of the struggle. The homefront experience was, after all, far less glorious by comparison, being characterized by persistently frayed nerves and punctuated not by gunfire but by emotional turmoil brought about by a consistent inundation of bad news and fear of an uncertain future. In the tumultuous, strife-filled climb back to a new normal, that part of the story became easily forgotten.[131]

"I Have Conducted Our Municipal Little Bark Through This Troublous Sea"

O n March 12, 1866, Eufaula mayor C.J. Pope addressed city council for the last time. His remarks upon leaving office were essentially a reflection on the upheaval that the town had experienced in the recently concluded war in whose long shadow the town still labored. Self-servingly, he reminded city leaders at the outset of "the multiplied difficulties" he encountered and the many "trials" to which he had been subjected during and after the Union occupation. According to Pope, his troubles only increased when the troops departed and left him to tend to "those matters growing out of the changed conditions of our country and thereby our changed relations to our freed population." He noted that "the freedman from fifty to one-hundred miles around the city of Eufaula, flocked here," and asserted that he labored tirelessly to inform them of "their true conditions and interest and the course best to be pursued by them, looking to their ultimate welfare." Citing the lack of violence in Eufaula in the disorderly aftermath of a war that shook the very foundations of Southern society to its core as the best proof of his effective leadership, he attempted to draw attention to "the success with which I have conducted our municipal little bark through this troublous sea." Attempting to put the events of the past four years into perspective, he closed by remarking that the experience had been "an ordeal, the like of which has seldom if ever been witnessed, by any people or any country since the dawn of civilization."[132]

While Pope's words read as Victorian hyperbole today, they certainly did not come off as such to many of his fellow citizens. In a very real sense, even at the time, his listeners knew that the Civil War marked the transition from one era to another—the death of one society and the birth of another. They, along with their friends and neighbors across the South, ultimately embarked on a long and tortured philosophical journey to discover what exactly it all meant. They largely settled on venerating the soldiers who fought for Southern independence as honorable patriots, choosing to remember the homefront hardships and worries as a mere sidelight, if at all—the minimum sacrifice that could have been made for a noble cause. Legend had it all borne quite cheerfully, to boot. In retrospect, this celebration of a constructed past probably did as much to create a twentieth-century southern identity as the political battles over slavery or the war itself.

The experience of civilians, both slave and free, if somewhat clouded by time and efforts to orchestrate the memory of the war, were nonetheless real, and the recollections were raw even decades later. Parthenia Hague remembered in her later years "how clearly even now I read every milestone of that convulsed period." Writing in 1930, Eugenia Persons Smartt offered perhaps the fullest quintessential expression of the "Lost Cause" spirit of remembrance of the war by recording in her history that Eufaula's citizens "love our country even as the Greeks with Leonidas loved Sparta. We love its flag, the glorious stars and stripes, the emblem of the free. We would revive no bitter memories which God has permitted to fade out from manly and fraternal hearts. We only remember what is pleasant and approved of God; valor, fidelity, self-devotion, and glorious loyalty to our native land. These we can never forget." In some ways, that is exactly the manner in which the war was remembered in Eufaula—and the South in general—for a long time. In some ways, it still is.[133]

Eufaula would slowly make a comeback from the setbacks of the war years. Stores reopened, river traffic returned and the town eventually began to grow again. A decade after Grierson's arrival, Eufaula had a population of five thousand and boasted some fifty brick stores. A vital and growing trading center recovering from the "dire effects of the late civil war," it was, in the words of one Reconstruction-era resident, rapidly on the way to again "blossom as the rose." While a blossoming did take place, it frankly occurred on a smaller scale than residents might have predicted. Eufaula remained a regionally important trading center for decades after the war, but by the turn of the twentieth century, its incremental growth paled in comparison to the relative boom being experienced in nearby Columbus, Montgomery and upstart Dothan.

Rather than foretelling a decline into oblivion, this pattern facilitated preservation of more of the town's architectural fabric than might otherwise have been possible, lending it a special charming character that made it unique indeed by the time of the centennial of the Civil War and the misguided "urban renewal" efforts of the era. Fortunately, the city recognized its opportunity and embraced its role as a scenic small town, forming a group dedicated to preserving its special heritage and launching the oldest and most successful tour of homes in Alabama, the annual Eufaula Pilgrimage, in 1965. Today, it is recognized as a community with a love of history and a remarkable preservation ethic. Even if it does not preserve or interpret all aspects of its past equally, choosing to market itself as encased in antebellum and Victorian amber, because of the vision of local citizens, opportunities continue to abound there that do not exist elsewhere.[134]

In 1904, Eufaula erected a monument dedicated to the memory of its Confederate heroes and the quest for Southern independence. Today, the granite sculpture of a solemn soldier adorning that edifice stands sentinel in the middle of one of the busiest intersections in town, the inscriptions praising the valor of Southern soldiers and the gloriousness of the Lost Cause virtually inaccessible and unreadable except by the most devoted passersby or those brave enough to venture to it on foot. It is, in a way, a fitting symbol for Eufaula's Civil War experience, for it is prominent and visible enough to all who pass through town to provide an aura of historical authenticity and somber commemoration, even if its details are simultaneously hidden in plain sight, ironically difficult to access and routinely overlooked.[135]

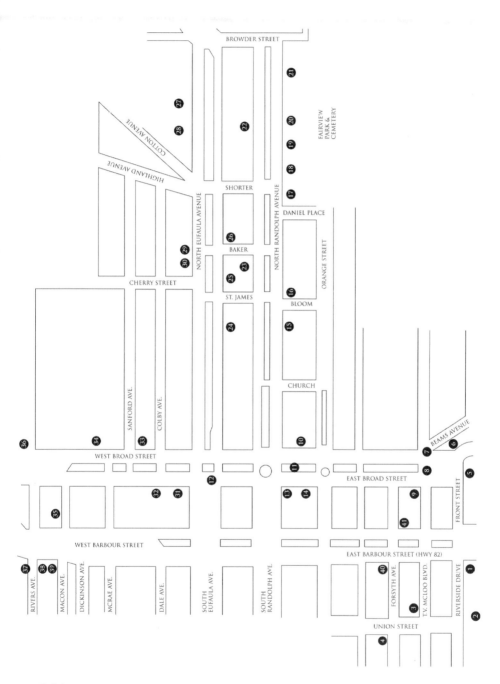

Driving tour map.

Appendix

Historic Site Tour

This driving tour will take you through the heart of Eufaula's historic
business and residential districts, highlighting homes, businesses and
historic sites significant to the city's Civil War years. I invite you to start
your tour on the bluff overlooking beautiful Lake Eufaula/Walter F. George
(formed in 1963) at Governor's Park on Riverside Drive. The park is
located just south of the intersection of Riverside Drive and Barbour Street
(Highway 82). You may park near the large cross in the parking lot just past
the park benches.

1. **Governor's Park** celebrates the eight governors of Alabama from
    Barbour County—the most of any county in the state—including
    Eufaula native Governor John Gill Shorter (1861–63). The park
    overlooks Lake Eufaula/Walter F. George, formed by the damming
    of the Chattahoochee River at Fort Gaines to the south. The lake
    covers more than forty-five thousand acres and has approximately
    640 miles of shoreline. At the time of the Civil War, the river ran
    directly below this bluff.

2. Proceed south on Riverside Drive to **Shorter Cemetery** (open by
    appointment only). This cemetery, situated near the location of the
    family home of pioneer Eufaula settler Reuben Shorter, dates to 1839.
    It contains the grave of Governor John Gill Shorter, who died in 1872.

Go back down Riverside Drive and turn left onto Union Street. Go up one block and turn right onto T.V. McCoo Boulevard. Turn around at the first break in the median (Christian Alley).

3. On the right is **St. Luke AME Church** (234 South T.V. McCoo Boulevard). This church, the oldest extant in Eufaula, was originally built in 1840 as the Eufaula Baptist Church. Pioneer settler Reuben Shorter donated the lumber for the structure and had his slaves dress it by hand. During the war, many of Eufaula's leading citizens worshiped here. When the original white  congregation outgrew the facility after the Civil War, the church was given to the Negro Baptist Church and later purchased by the AME congregation.

4. Proceed to Union Street and take a right. Go up one block. On the left corner of Union Street and Forsyth Avenue is the **Buford-Jackson House** (306 Forsyth Avenue). Firebrand secessionist Jefferson Buford, who personally underwrote most of the expenses related to the failed proslavery settlement in Kansas in 1856, built this home circa 1845.

Take a right onto Forsyth Avenue and then turn right onto Barbour Street (Highway 82). Get into the left lane. At Riverside Drive, just before crossing the bridge, turn left.

5. On the end of the block on the right is **The Tavern** (105 Front Street). The oldest existing building in Eufaula, this structure was built in 1836. Originally an inn, it has served as a residence, church and business over the years. During the Civil War, it was pressed into service as a Confederate hospital.

6. Directly ahead is the **Wellborn House** (630 East Broad Street). Built in 1839 on Livingston Avenue by Dr. Thomas Levi Wellborn, this home was moved to its current location in 1971. It is believed to

be among the first Greek Revival homes built in the Eufaula area. Dr. Wellborn was a physician and served on the staff of his brother, General William Wellborn, during the Second Creek War (1836–37). The family remained prominent in the area for generations.

Follow Riverside Drive up to the five-point intersection.

7. To the right is Beams Drive, which leads to the U.S. Army Corps of Engineer Office. This road follows closely the original route to the covered bridge that spanned the Chattahoochee River during the Civil War and the steamboat landing. The bridge that stood here during the Civil War was built by master craftsmen Horace King, who had been born a slave. The landing was the location for the docking of steamboats, where cotton was loaded and trade goods brought into town. It was also the place where crowds gathered to send off troops leaving for the war. Feel free to drive down to the Corps Office parking lot at the end of the road and return to the intersection.

8. While the exact location is unknown, **Will Young's machine shop**, which assisted in the naval construction activities upriver in Columbus, stood on a street corner in this vicinity.

9. Opposite the post office on Broad Street is the **Milton-Jones House** (525 East Broad). James Milton built this Italianate cottage in about 1850.

Proceed west on Broad Street. You will pass **Confederate Park** in the median on your left, which contains a stone marker commemorating the route of a branch of the Jefferson Davis Highway, a transcontinental road planned in the 1910s that ran through Eufaula. A double row of sycamore trees lined this wide street during the war era. You will advance past Livingston, Orange and Randolph Avenues, ending up at Eufaula Avenue. The first letters of the names of these thoroughfares spell out L-O-R-E in honor of Seth Lore, who assisted in laying out the town in the 1830s. Beginning about where the modern post office is and stretching up to Randolph Avenue was a section of town known locally as "Rotten Row" during the Civil War era. This block contained some of the oldest businesses in town during the war. Virtually all were wooden and in various stages of decay at the time. The block between Randolph and Eufaula Avenues, containing newer brick structures during the Civil War years, was known as "Brick Row."

10. In the block between Orange and Randolph Avenues stood the **offices of the *Eufaula Spirit of the South***, the organ of the secessionist faction the Eufaula Regency. In both this block and the block between Randolph and Eufaula Avenues stood several of the city's wartime law offices in which some of the leading proponents of Southern nationalism were employed.

11. According to local legend, **slave auctions** were commonly held in the vicinity where the gazebo now stands in the median of the block between Orange and Randolph Avenues.

Proceed to Eufaula Avenue in the left hand lane and turn around to head down the south side of Broad Street.

12. Directly ahead as you turn will be the **Confederate Monument**. Presented by the United Daughters of the Confederacy in 1904, the monument occupies the middle of the intersection of Broad Street and Eufaula Avenue. Unlike many similar monuments, which feature a statue of a Confederate soldier facing north, Eufaula's sentinel faces east toward the Chattahoochee River—the direction from which most wartime city residents believed an attack would come.

13. On the corner of Randolph Avenue and Broad Street is the **McNab Bank–Lewis Agency** (201 East Broad Street). During the Civil War, this building housed John McNab's Eastern National Bank. It is one of the oldest bank buildings in the state. An Italianate structure, it features ornamental iron on the front, side, entry steps and railing.

14. Just a few doors down on the same block is the **Ramser-Satterwhite Building** (215 East Broad), an 1840s Italianate commercial structure. During the Civil War era, the Swiss immigrant Ramser family operated a furniture and cabinet shop here.

At the intersection of Broad and Orange, turn left, back onto Broad Street and go back up to Randolph Avenue. Take a right onto North Randolph Avenue.

15. Just past the First Presbyterian Church is the **Bray-Garrison House** (211 North Randolph Avenue). This Gothic Revival house was built by New England native John Bray in about 1855. It originally sat one lot to the south, closer to the church, but was moved to make way for the garden with a central fountain that now occupies the space.

16. On the next block is the **Smartt-Parker-Comer House** (315 North Randolph Avenue). Early settler Alexander McDonald built this house

in 1838 on the site of a log stockade constructed for the protection of town residents during the Second Creek War. Part of the fort walls are incorporated into its design.

17. On the next block is the **Pugh-Wilkinson House** (501 North Randolph Avenue). Noted Regency member and prominent politician James L. Pugh built this Folk Victorian home in 1855. Pugh was serving in the U.S. House of Representatives at the time of secession. He served briefly as a Confederate military officer

before winning election to the Confederate Congress, in which he served until the end of the war. After his citizenship was restored, he later served in the U.S. Senate.

18. Two doors down is **Dean-Page Hall** (539 North Randolph Avenue). Constructed in 1850 by city councilman William T. Simpson, the home was named by his daughter Caroline (Mrs. L.Y. Dean).

19. Next will be the **Rhodes-Winkleblack House** (619 North Randolph Avenue). This home was built in 1853 by Elizabeth Rhodes, whose diary is quoted from extensively in this volume, and her husband, Chauncey Rhodes.

20. A short distance farther down Randolph Avenue is the **Milton-MacElvain House** (725 North Randolph Avenue). Built in circa

1850 by Mr. N.M. Hyatt, it was purchased in 1871 by local jeweler and optician James Milton.

21. A short distance from the intersection of North Randolph Avenue and Browder Street is **Fairview Cemetery**. You may drive into the cemetery and tour by car or on foot. Established in the 1830s, this is Eufaula's oldest cemetery. Many of the town's early citizens, including several prominent during the Civil War era, are buried here. In the cemetery are graves for dozens of Eufaula-area Confederate veterans,

as well as many of those who died in local hospitals, and the graves of slaves. The iron fencing around the cemetery entrance is from Union Female College.

Proceed to Browder Street, take a U-turn onto Randolph and head south.

22. A short distance down on the right will be the **Macon-Thomas House** (606 North Randolph Avenue). Built circa 1850, this Greek Revival house was occupied by the builders of Dean-Page Hall during its construction. The dining room and porch were added later.

23. Just past the intersection with Baker Street is the **Thornton-Rudderman-Gulledge House** (312 North Randolph Avenue). Dr. William Thornton and his wife, Mary B. Shorter Thornton, built this home in about 1845. Thornton was Eufaula's first mayor. Although the veranda has been added, the interior, including imported cathedral doors, remains virtually unchanged.

At the intersection with Broad Street, take a right and go up one block. Take a right onto North Eufaula Avenue (Highway 431).

24. The first house on your right will be the **Hart House**, headquarters office of the Historic Chattahoochee Commission (211 North Eufaula Avenue). New Hampshire native and early Eufaula settler John Hart built the home before 1850. It was occupied by his descendants for nearly a century. Today, the home serves as an office for the commission, a bi-state agency that promotes heritage tourism, history education and historic preservation, and as a regional visitor information center. It is open to the public on weekdays.

25. Just past St. James Episcopal Church is the **Couric-Smith House** (325 North Eufaula Avenue). French immigrant Charles M. Couric built this Greek Revival home in about 1845, when this neighborhood was on the outskirts of town and featured only a few country estates. Additions were made to the home in the 1890s.

26. A few doors down is the **Bray-Barron House** (411 North Eufaula Avenue). The home was constructed in 1850 by Nathan Bray, one of four brothers from New England who moved to Eufaula around that time. Several members of the Bray family served in the Confederate army.

Proceed to the break in the median dividing Eufaula Avenue immediately before you reach Browder Street and turn around to head south toward downtown.

27. On the right is the **Conner-Taylor House** (720 North Eufaula Avenue). Believed to have been built in 1863 by William M. Raney, this house is one of the very few completed during the war. It underwent significant alteration in the early 1900s.

28. A few houses down is the **Drewery-Mitchell-Moorer House** (640 North Eufaula Avenue). The Italianate home was built by physician John Drewery, noted for his ability to treat typhoid. The

home was used as a hospital during severe typhoid outbreaks. During the Civil War, wounded soldiers were cared for on the large latticed back porch. A belvedere originally topped the house, but it burned in 1914 and was not replaced.

29. Next is **Shorter Mansion** (340 North Eufaula Avenue), the headquarters of the Eufaula Heritage Association and the home of the Eufaula History Museum. The museum contains a variety of artifacts

from the city's past, including several items dating to the Civil War era. The home was built in 1884 by Eli Sims Shorter II, the son of Regency member Eli Shorter, and his wife, Wileyna Lamar Shorter. It underwent significant remodeling in the early 1900s. The home is open for tours Monday through Saturday.

30. Next door is the **Wingate-Dozier House** (334 North Eufaula Avenue). Built in 1846 by Elias Miller, it was later owned by the

noted secessionist John Cochran and served as a meeting place for the Eufaula Regency. Later, it was owned by steamboat captain Hezekiah Wingate. Originally built in the Greek Revival style, the home underwent significant remodeling in the 1890s and now appears Victorian.

Proceed to the intersection of Eufaula Avenue and Broad Street and take a right at the Confederate Monument. You will be driving up College Hill, so named for Union Female College that stood on the crest of the hill at the time of the Civil War. This road was the route through which Union troopers entered town in April 1865. It was known at the time as the "Clayton Road."

31. Across the street from the Piggly Wiggly once stood the **Battle-Spurlock House**. On the front porch of the home, which closely resembled the White House of the Confederacy in Montgomery, musician J.C. Van Houten sat and played "Dixie" as the Union troops marched into town.

32. One door down from the Holleman-Foy Mansion on the left is the **Sparks-Irby House** (257 West Broad Street). The home was

owned by Henry C. Hart at the time of the Civil War. Hart traded it to Henry R. Shorter after the war for sixty thousand pounds of cotton. Alabama governor Chauncey Sparks (1943–47) later lived here.

33. At the end of the next block, on the right, is the **Copeland-Savage House** (420 West Broad Street). E.C. Joyce built this Greek Revival cottage-style home in 1851. It was extensively remodeled after the war.

34. A short distance up the hill on the right is **Kendall Manor** (534

West Broad Street), perhaps Eufaula's most magnificent home. James Turner Kendall built this Italian Renaissance home, which remained in his family until 1990. Construction began on the home in 1860 but was delayed due to the war, and it was not finished until 1872.

35. Immediately past Kendall Manor, in the median of West Broad Street, is a historic marker commemorating the arrival of General Benjamin H. Grierson's cavalry in Eufaula on April 29, 1865.

36. Just ahead on the right is the site of **Union Female College**, founded a few years prior to the war through the efforts of local fraternal organizations.

Proceed to Rivers Avenue and turn left.

37. Directly ahead on the right is **St. Mary's on the Hill** (206 Rivers Avenue). Built by local merchant Charles Laney, the Italianate home originally served as a Catholic retreat.

Turn left onto Barbour Street.

38. On the right is **Fendall Hall** (917 West Barbour Street). Prominent local businessman Edward B. Young built this Italianate home in 1860. Anna Young, whose letters are featured in this book, lived here

during the war. She and her husband, Hubert Dent, a Confederate veteran, later lived here. During the war, the house was known by the family simply as "the house on the hill." A granddaughter of the builders first referred to it as Fendall Hall around the 1940s. The home is now a historic site operated by the Alabama Historical Commission and is open for tours during posted hours.

39. One door down on the right is the **Cato-Thorne House** (823 West Barbour Street). Built by leading attorney and Regency member Lewis Lewellen Cato, the home was often a meeting place for local secessionists. A large party attended by several  local leaders took place here upon the announcement of Alabama's departure from the Union.

Continue down Barbour Street to downtown and cross Eufaula Avenue (Highway 431).

40. Four blocks down on the right will be **White's Funeral Home** (441 East Barbour Street). Built in 1840 by Dr. William L. Cowan, it was purchased after the war by merchant Jacob Ramser.

41. On the left, on the corner of the next block, is the **Sheppard Cottage** (504 East Barbour Street). This home, built in 1837 in the Tidewater Cottage style, is Eufaula's oldest remaining home. It was built by early settler Henry A. Field.

Notes

Preface

1. Biographical information on Hague taken from Denney, *Distaff Civil War*, 40, and Frank, *Women in the American Civil War*, 320. I have chosen to refer to Hague in the narrative by her married name, under which she published her book. Full citations for the books mentioned are: Parthenia Hague, *A Blockaded Family: Life in Southern Alabama During the Civil War* (Carlisle, MA: Applewood Books, 1995); *The Diaries of Elizabeth Rhodes: Depicting Her Life and Times in the South from 1858 to 1900* (Dothan: Image Agency, 2013); Victoria Clayton, *White and Black Under the Old Regime* (Milwaukee: Young Churchman Company, 1899); Gerald Ray Mathis, *John Horry Dent: South Carolina Aristocrat on the Alabama Frontier* (Tuscaloosa: University of Alabama Press, 1979); and Charles M. Crook, *Fendall Hall: A True Story of Good Times and Bad Times on the Chattahoochee River* (Charles M. Crook, 2004). Hyatt's unpublished diary is in private possession.

Introduction

2. *Macon Telegraph*, February 7, 1861.
3. There are several histories of Eufaula that informed this summary of the town's history. These include Crook, *Fendall Hall*; Dorman, *History of Barbour County*; Flewellen, *Along Broad Street*; Smartt, *History of Eufaula*; Thompson, *History of Barbour County*; and Walker, *Backtracking in Barbour County*.
4. Flewellen, *Along Broad Street*, 27–28; Eufaula City Council Minutes Record Book for 1847–57. In an article that appeared in the *Columbus Enquirer* on January 11, 1843, it was explained that the name change was not meant as a slight to General Irwin. Rather, it was selected because it "told of other times." Legend holds that it was prominent Eufaula businessman Edward Young who prompted the change after having lost a particularly large sum of money through having mail misdirected.
5. Census information taken from University of Virginia Historical Census Browser for 1860, http://mapserver.lib.virginia.edu; *Macon Telegraph*, April 3, 1861. The city's important role in the vibrant antebellum river trade is chronicled in a number of histories of the city and region. Ed Mueller's seminal study, *Perilous Journeys*, contains a wealth of information gathered from area newspapers chronicling this rise.
6. *Eufaula Express*, July 11, 1861; *Eufaula Spirit of South*, August 27, 1861; September 10, 1861; and June 30, 1863; Carey, *Sold Down the River*, 188; "List of Merchants" in Eufaula Athenaeum Collection.
7. Flewellen, *Along Broad Street*, 28–45, 86; Williams, *Rich Man's War*, 14; quote from Battle in Beck, *Third Alabama!*, 23.
8. *Eufaula Express*, December 22, 1859.

Chapter 1

9. Flewellen, *Along Broad Street*, 59; Jennings, *Nashville Convention*; Walther, *William L. Yancey*, 128; DuBose, *Life and Times of William Lowndes Yancey*, 252; Moore, *History of Alabama*, 244–45; Denman, *Secession Movement in Alabama*, 48–48; Thornton, *Politics and Power in a Slave Society*, 239, 252–53; Perry, *Conceived in Liberty*, 81.

10. Walker, *Backtracking in Barbour County*, 161; Barney, *Secessionist Impulse*, xv. For biographical summaries of the Regency's membership, see Barney, *Secessionist Impulse*.

11. For a more detailed account of the formation, functioning and influence of the Regency, see Bunn, *"Eufaula Regency."* The name "Eufaula Regency" made its first appearance in the historiography of the secession movement with the publication of Lewy Dorman's *Party Politics in Alabama from 1850 through 1860*. Dorman did not cite a specific source, only noting that local Unionists probably coined the term in denigration of what they saw as the group's presumption to speak for all of Barbour County's citizens. No evidence has surfaced that any members of the group referred to themselves with the term, and no historian who has written on the topic since Dorman has discovered a more definitive source for the sobriquet.

12. *Eufaula Spirit of the South*, October 15, 1850, and October 22, 1850.

13. Smartt, *History of Eufaula*, 61.

14. Dorman, *History of Barbour County*, 187; *Eufaula Spirit of the South*, May 13 and 20, 1851; *Eufaula Southern Shield*, October 23, 1851.

15. For a brief summary of the campaign and its aftermath, see DuBose, *Life and Times of William Lowndes Yancey*, 264–65; Walker, *Backtracking in Barbour County*, 165; Dorman, *History of Barbour County*, 189.

16. Troup apparently only accepted the nomination to help organize the State-Rights (or Southern) Party. In his letter to the nominating committee, he made it clear that, at the age of seventy-two, he could only accept the nomination for "the sole purpose" of organizing the party. Quitman accepted his nomination as a symbolic act to assist in the development of the party, as well. For information on the campaign, see Hodgson, *Cradle of the Confederacy*, 334; Harden, *Life of George M. Troup*, 529–30; Claiborne, *Life and Correspondence of John A. Quitman*, 185; May, *John A. Quitman*, 267–68; Walther, *William L. Yancey*, 142–43; Walther, *Fire-Eaters*, 106–7; Rachleff, "Racial Fear and Political Factionalism," 193.

17. The most detailed account of the Buford expedition is found in Fleming, "Buford Expedition to Kansas," 38–48. See also Clayton, *White and Black Under the Old Regime*. The wife of Buford's friend Henry D. Clayton, Mrs. Clayton accompanied her husband to Kansas and recorded a brief version of the history of the expedition in her memoirs. Buford's expedition stopped in Columbus, Georgia, a few days after departing Eufaula, where it rendezvoused with additional recruits before heading on to Montgomery and boarding a steamer.

18. Fleming, "Buford Expedition to Kansas."

19. *Eufaula Express*, November 18, 1858; Williams, *Rich Man's War*, 45–46. The masthead of the *Banner* had changed by February 1860.

Chapter 2

20. Smartt, *History of Eufaula*, 62–66; Flewellen, *Along Broad Street*, 71.

21. Quotes from Webb and Armbrester, *Alabama Governors*, 71, and *Montgomery Weekly Advertiser*, December 12, 1860.

22. *Montgomery Daily Mail*, December 5, 1860.

23. Eufaula Heritage Association, *Diaries of Elizabeth Rhodes*, 84; Crook, *Fendall Hall*, 100; Lizzie Buford to Anna Mercur, December 17, 1860, in Anna Mercur Papers, Southern Historical Collection.

24. Smartt, *History of Eufaula*, 68. Accounts of this ride, with varying degrees of detail, are recounted in several histories of Eufaula.

25. Eufaula Heritage Association, *Diaries of Elizabeth Rhodes*, 90–91; Dorman, *History of Barbour County*, 210; Walker, *Backtracking in Barbour County*, 139.

26. Eufaula Heritage Association, *Diaries of Elizabeth Rhodes*, 90–91; Smartt, *History of Eufaula*, 66.

27. Eufaula Heritage Association, *Diaries of Elizabeth Rhodes*, 88, 93; Crook, *Fendall Hall*, 102.

28. Clayton, *Black and White Under the Old Regime*, 88–89; Davidson, "James Lawrence Pugh," 30–32.

29. Anna Mercur Papers, Southern Historical Collection, December 17, 1860; Eufaula Heritage Association, *Diaries of Elizabeth Rhodes*, 84, 96; Hague, *Blockaded Family*, 4; Mathis, *John Horry Dent*, 200.

30. Davis, *Government of Our Own*, 8, 20–21; Anderson, *Federalism, Secession and the American State*, 111–12.

31. John Wilhoydt Lewis Daniel, who later served in the Confederate army, was Barbour County's other delegate to the secession convention. Walther, *William L. Yancey*, 281. For a discussion of the proceedings of the secession convention, see Darden, "Alabama Secession Convention," 287–356. By most counts, those favoring immediate secession held a fifty-three to forty-seven majority as the convention began.

32. Smith, *History and Debates*, 397, 417.

33. Eufaula Heritage Association, *Diaries of Elizabeth Rhodes*, 96; Dorman, *History of Barbour County*, 209; Flewellen, *Along Broad Street*, 70–72; Hyatt diary.

34. Davis, *Government of Our Own*, 124, 149–50; Brannen, "John Gill Shorter," 10.

35. McMillan, *Disintegration of a Confederate State*; Brannen, "John Gill Shorter," 18–19; Webb and Armbrester, *Alabama Governors*, 71; Fleming, *Civil War and Reconstruction in Alabama*, 131.

Chapter 3

36. Detzer, *Allegiance*, 268–69.

37. Dorman, *History of Barbour County*, 207, 230; Hyatt diary; *Macon Telegraph*, February 7, 1861.

38. Smartt, *History of Eufaula*, 65, 67, 70; Walker, *Backtracking in Barbour County*, 216; Perry, *Conceived in Liberty*, 110; *Eufaula Spirit of the South*, September 10, 1861.

39. Crook, *Fendall Hall*, 100; Dorman, *History of Barbour County*, 210; Barrow, Segars and Rosenburg, *Black Confederates*, 9.

40. Hague, *Blockaded Family*, 41.

41. Dorman, *History of Barbour County*, 218–19; Walker, *Backtracking in Barbour County*, 213; Flewellen, *Along Broad Street*, 76; Smartt, *History of Eufaula*, 71; McCorries, *History of the First Regiment*.

42. McMillan, *Disintegration of a Confederate State*, 210; Clayton, *Black and White Under the Old Regime*, 91; Davidson, "James Lawrence Pugh," 35.

43. Troop departures from Eufaula are discussed in several histories. See particularly Dorman, *History of Barbour County*, 214–27; Smartt, *History of Eufaula*; and Eufaula Heritage Association, *Diaries of Elizabeth Rhodes*, 98.

44. Eufaula Heritage Association, *Diaries of Elizabeth Rhodes*, 43; Dorman, *History of Barbour County*, 228; Hyatt diary.

45. Crook, *Fendall Hall*, 105; Napier, "Martial Montgomery," 129; Smartt, *History of Eufaula*, 72.

46. Mathis, *In the Land of the Living*, 2; Walker, *Backtracking in Barbour County*, 215; Crook, *Fendall Hall*, 158; Dorman, *History of Barbour County*, 224.

47. Crook, *Fendall Hall*, 159; Dorman, *History of Barbour County*, 230; Smartt, *History of Eufaula*, 74; George, *Brown University*, 26.

48. Crook, *Fendall Hall*, 118, 243, 275; Clayton, *Black and White Under the Old Regime*, 94, 131; Owens, "History of Eufaula, Alabama," 70.

49. Eufaula Heritage Association, *Diaries of Elizabeth Rhodes*, 113; Crook, *Fendall Hall*, 140–41.

50. Crook, *Fendall Hall*, 113, 116, 131, 135–36.

51. Ibid., 158; Dorman, *History of Barbour County*, 225–28; *Baltimore Sun*, April 22, 1865.

52. *Eufaula Spirit of the South*, June 28, 1863; Dorman, *History of Barbour County*, 228.

53. Eufaula Heritage Association, *Diaries of Elizabeth Rhodes*, 143, 146, 156, 172, 177.

54. Dorman, *History of Barbour County*, 225; Owens, "History of Eufaula, Alabama," 63; Crook, *Fendall Hall*, 276–77.

55. Clayton, *Black and White Under the Old Regime*, 139.

56. Crook, *Fendall Hall*, 291–92; Mathis, *In the Land of the Living*, 107.

57. Eufaula Heritage Association, *Diaries of Elizabeth Rhodes*, 130; Hague, *Blockaded Family*, 130, 141.

Chapter 4

58. Eufaula Heritage Association, *Diaries of Elizabeth Rhodes*, 127.

59. United States War Department, *War of the Rebellion* (hereafter U.S. War Department, *Official Records*), series IV, vol. 1, part 1, 32, 49; *Eufaula Spirit of the South*, August 28, 1863.

60. *Eufaula Express*, July 11, 1861; *Eufaula Spirit of the South*, September 10, 1861; Eufaula Heritage Association, *Historic Eufaula*.

61. Owens, "History of Eufaula, Alabama," 63; Mathis, *John Horry Dent*, 199, 201; Williams, *Rich Man's War*, 126.

62. Mathis, *John Horry Dent*, 201; Owens, "History of Eufaula, Alabama," 69; Flewellen, *Along Broad Street*, 78; Hague, *Blockaded Family*, 24–25; Clayton, *Black and White Under the Old Regime*, 123; U.S. War Department, *Official Records*, series I, vol. 14, part 1, 680; Eufaula Heritage Association, *Diaries of Elizabeth Rhodes*, 167–68.

63. Dorman, *History of Barbour County*, 228; Mueller, *Perilous Journeys*, 103; Flewellen, *Along Broad Street*, 78; Hague, *Blockaded Family*, 130; Crook, *Fendall Hall*, 161.

64. Mueller, *Perilous Journeys*, 104–8, 116; *Eufaula Spirit of the South*, June 23, 1863; Dorman, *History of Barbour County*, 230.

65. Hague, *Blockaded Family*, 91–92.

66. *Eufaula Spirit of the South*, June 28 and June 30, 1863; Mathis, *John Horry*

Dent, 206–7; Williams, *Rich Man's War*, 83; Eufaula Heritage Association, *Diaries of Elizabeth Rhodes*, 172.

67. Crook, *Fendall Hall*, 161; Smartt, *History of Eufaula*, 91.

68. Eufaula Heritage Association, *Diaries of Elizabeth Rhodes*, 121; Hague, *Blockaded Family*, 15.

69. Hague, *Blockaded Family*, 17, 26; Walker, *Backtracking in Barbour County*, 188; Clayton, *Black and White Under the Old Regime*, 116; Williams, *Rich Man's War*, 33; Mathis, *John Horry Dent*, 206–7.

70. Hague, *Blockaded Family*, 36, 38, 40, 42, 47, 53, 68, 104. See also Walker, *Backtracking in Barbour County*, 189–90; Clayton, *Black and White Under the Old Regime*, 199, 121; Mathis, *John Horry Dent*, 208; Flewellen, *Along Broad Street*, 80.

71. Hague, *Blockaded Family*, 46–47; Clayton, *Black and White Under the Old Regime*, 117; *Eufaula Spirit of the South*, September 10, 1861; Flewellen, *Along Broad Street*, 81.

72. Hague, *Blockaded Family*, 57, 106–7; Clayton, *Black and White Under the Old Regime*, 113; Walker, *Backtracking in Barbour County*, 188.

73. Hague, *Blockaded Family*, 37; Mathis, *John Horry Dent*, 203.

74. Hague, *Blockaded Family*, 24–27, 101; Eufaula Heritage Association, *Diaries of Elizabeth Rhodes*, 123; Hyatt diary; Smartt, *History of Eufaula*, 72; Mathis, *John Horry Dent*, 199.

75. Flewellen, *Along Broad Street*, 79; Eufaula Heritage Association, *Diaries of Elizabeth Rhodes*, 159; Mathis, *John Horry Dent*, 210; Davis, *Rhett*, 540–42.

76. Hague, *Blockaded Family*, 48–49, 87–88.

77. Clayton, *Black and White Under the Old Regime*, 103–4, 139; Eufaula Heritage Association, *Diaries of Elizabeth Rhodes*, 176; Hyatt diary; Mathis, *John Horry Dent*, 205; Dorman, *History of Barbour County*, 230; McKiven, "John Gill Shorter"; McMillan, *Disintegration of a Confederate State*.

78. Eufaula Heritage Association, *Diaries of Elizabeth Rhodes*, 151, 175; Hague, *Blockaded Family*, 119; *Albany Patriot*, May 19, 1864; *Eufaula Spirit of the South*, June 23, 28 and 30, 1863; Mathis, *John Horry Dent*, 207; LaFantasie, *Gettysburg Requiem*, 153; Crook, *Fendall Hall*, 276–77. The real name of "Blind Tom" was Thomas Bethune Wiggins.

79. *Columbus Enquirer*, January 15, 1861; *Andersonville Intelligencer*, April 4, 1861; Owens, "History of Eufaula," 71; Crook, *Fendall Hall*, 258, 276–77.

80. For information on slavery in the regional economy and social structure, see Carey, *Sold Down the River*; census information derived from Historical Census Browser from the University of Virginia, Geospatial and Statistical Data Center, http://mapserver.lib.virginia.edu/collections.

NOTES TO PAGES 75–86

81. Interviews with former slaves Matilda Pugh Daniel and Lizzie Hill, Federal Writer's Project, United States Work Projects Administration, Manuscript Division, Library of Congress; Eufaula Heritage Association, *Diaries of Elizabeth Rhodes*, 98–99.
82. George, *Brown University*, 23; Hague, *Blockaded Family*, 121.
83. Clayton, *Black and White Under the Old Regime*, 99, 116; Flewellen, *Along Broad Street*, 82; George, *Brown University*, 25; Dorman, *History of Barbour County*, 239.
84. Interview with former slave Gus Askew, Federal Writer's Project; Booth, *Cyclopedia of Colored Baptists*, 69–70.
85. Williams, *Weren't No Good Times*, 16–17; interview with former slave Theodore Fontaine Stewart, Federal Writer's Project; Smartt, *History of Eufaula*, 80; Burton, *Memories of Childhood Slavery Days*, 9.

Chapter 5

86. Smartt, *History of Eufaula*, 62; Flewellen, *Along Broad Street*, 81; Dorman, *History of Barbour County*, 225, 230, 242.
87. Owens, "History of Eufaula," 69; Dorman, *History of Barbour County*, 230; Crook, *Fendall Hall*, 160; U.S. War Department, *Official Records*, series I, vol. 15, part 1, 947–48; Williams, *Rich Man's War*, 131.
88. Mueller, *Perilous Journeys*, 104–5; United States Naval War Records Office, *Official Records of the Union and Confederate Navies* (hereafter U.S. Naval War Records Office, *Official Records*), series I, vol. 17, 857; Flewellen, *Along Broad Street*, 85; Dorman, *History of Barbour County*, 225. See also Turner, *Navy Gray*. The navigational aids sent for safekeeping in Eufaula were returned to Apalachicola at the end of the war.
89. Turner, *Navy Gray*, 78.
90. Turner, *Navy Gray*, 78–79; Mueller, *Perilous Journeys*, 107–8; U.S. War Department, *Official Records*, series I, vol. 14, part 1, 542–46. For information on the obstructions placed in the Apalachicola, which included the hulls of old steamboats and chains stretched across the river, see Mabelitini, "Confederate Fortification of the Apalachicola River."
91. *Clayton Banner*, May 31, 1860, and April 11, 1861; *Eufaula Spirit of the South*, August 27, 1861. There are virtually no advertisements for Young's business in Eufaula papers after 1861, perhaps indicating that he was

concentrating on fulfilling his contracts with Confederate authorities in Columbus.

92. Turner, *Navy Gray*, 158, 166, 268–74, 280–91, 298; Crook, *Fendall Hall*, 168, 173.

93. Turner, *Navy Gray*, 166, 206; Campbell, *Voices of the Confederate Navy*, 99; U.S. Naval War Records Office, *Official Records*, series I, vol. 17, 874; Crook, *Fendall Hall*, 174.

94. Mueller, *Perilous Journeys*, 113–14; Turner, *Navy Gray*, 187–93.

95. U.S. War Department, *Official Records*, series I, vol. 35, part 2, 165–66.

96. Flannery, *Civil War Pharmacy*, 172; Williams, *Rich Man's War*, 75; Schroeder-Lein, *Confederate Hospitals on the Move*.

97. Walker, *Backtracking in Barbour County*, 204–5; Crook, *Fendall Hall*, 329; Flewellen, *Along Broad Street*, 85; Schroeder-Lein, *Confederate Hospitals on the Move*, 104; Dorman, *History of Barbour County*, 225.

98. Schroeder-Lein, *Confederate Hospitals on the Move*, 111–12; Walker, *Backtracking in Barbour County*, 205.

99. Tucker, *Brigadier General John D. Imboden*, 280–81; Isham, *Care of Prisoners of War*, 21; Imboden, "Treatment of Prisoners," 193–95; Speer, *War of Vengeance*, 135. For information on the prison, see Marvel, *Andersonville*.

Chapter 6

100. Grierson's movements are chronicled in Dinges and Leckie, *Just and Righteous Cause*. Wilson's campaign is detailed in Jones, *Yankee Blitzkrieg*, and Misulia, *Columbus, Georgia*.

101. Flewellen, *Along Broad Street*, 87; Andrews, *War-Time Journal*, 145.

102. Horn et al., *Yankees Are Coming!*, 40; Walker, *Backtracking in Barbour County*, 201–2; U.S. War Department, *Official Records*, series I, vol. 49, part 2, 468–69; Dorman, *History of Barbour County*, 242–44.

103. Dinges and Leckie, *Just and Righteous Cause*, 335.

104. Clayton, *Black and White Under the Old Regime*, 144–49; Walker, *Backtracking in Barbour County*, 203; Horn et al., *Yankees Are Coming!*, 43–48. Colonel Whitfield Clark, a Confederate officer at home on leave, purportedly brought Clayton's vulnerable position to the attention of Grierson. Clayton probably just saw the glint off the troopers' carbines, as it is unlikely that they rode with bayonets mounted.

105. Horn et al., *Yankees Are Coming!*, 48. Information on Private Marlin obtained through the Soldier and Sailors Database, National Park Service, http://www.nps.gov/civilwar/soldiers-and-sailors-database.htm; Walmsley, *Experiences of a Civil War Horse-Soldier*, 151; Dorman, *History of Barbour County*, 246. The fallen Union soldier's body was later exhumed for reburial in his home state.

106. Walmsley, *Experiences of a Civil War Horse-Soldier*, 151–52; Dinges and Leckie, *Just and Righteous Cause*, 335.

107. Hague, *Blockaded Family*, 143–51.

108. Interview with former slave Maugan Shepherd, Federal Writer's Project; Hague, *Blockaded Family*, 152; Burton, *Memories of Childhood Slavery Days*, 9.

109. Hague, *Blockaded Family*, 144–46; Smartt, *History of Eufaula*, 79–80; Clayton, *Black and White Under the Old Regime*, 144–46.

110. Hague, *Blockaded Family*, 155, 159; U.S. War Department, *Official Records*, series I, vol. 49, part 1, 302. Grierson claimed in his reports to have taken special precaution to not burn any of the estimated 300,000 bales of cotton he passed, as he believed that the crop would very soon "find its way to market and come under the control of the Government" anyway. He further claimed, perhaps with some degree of exaggeration, that all along his route "private property, except where it was necessary for the sustenance of men and horses, was respected; and immediately upon the receipt of the news of an armistice between Sherman and Johnston, as also of the suspension of hostilities pending the surrender of General Dick Taylor, the most stringent orders were issued and enforced forbidding the impressment of stock, and vouchers were given for all subsistence stores taken."

111. Crook, *Fendall Hall*, 388; Walker, *Backtracking in Barbour County*, 204; Horn et al., *Yankees Are Coming!*, 53.

112. Horn et al., *Yankees Are Coming!*, 53; Walker, *Backtracking in Barbour County*, 204; Hinges and Leckie, *Just and Righteous Cause*, 336–37; Crook, *Fendall Hall*, 387; Dorman, *History of Barbour County*, 245; Smartt, *History of Eufaula*, 79–80.

113. Hinges and Leckie, *Just and Righteous Cause*, 335–36; Horn et al., *Yankees Are Coming!*, 55; Smartt, *History of Eufaula*, 80.

114. Hinges and Leckie, *Just and Righteous Cause*, 336; Horn et al., *Yankees Are Coming!*, 55; Dorman, *History of Barbour County*, 248; Smartt, *History of Eufaula*, 79; U.S. War Department, *Official Records*, series I, vol. 49, part 2, 562.

115. Owen, *Report of the Alabama History Commission*, 90–91. Portions of the records may have been sent all the way to Augusta, Georgia. Taylor is

listed as secretary to the governor in Eufaula newspaper articles during the war.

116. McMillan, *Disintegration of a Confederate State*, 119–20; McMillan, *Alabama Confederate Reader*, 418; Williams, *Rich Man's War*, 17; Yearns, *Confederate Governors*, 239, note 99.

Chapter 7

117. U.S. War Department, *Official Records*, series I, vol. 49, part 2, 562.

118. Walmsley, *Experiences of a Civil War Horse-Soldier*, 152; U.S. War Department, *Official Records*, series I, vol. 49, part 2, 533, 562, 580, 583–85; letter from Headquarters Detachment, Third Brigade Cavalry, to Lt. Beach, May 3, 1865, Eufaula Athenaeum.

119. U.S. War Department, *Official Records*, series I, vol. 49, part 1, 300–302; Walker, *Backtracking in Barbour County*, 205; Dorman, *History of Barbour County*, 248; Williams, *Rich Man's War*, 183; Smartt, *History of Eufaula*, 80.

120. Owen, *Report of the Alabama History Commission*, 91; Walker, *Backtracking in Barbour County*, 223–24; Dorman, *History of Barbour County*, 249. As late as 2010, two state ledgers presumed to be among those sent to Eufaula were located in town and returned to the Alabama Department of Archives and History.

121. Turner, *Navy Gray*, 177, 187–88, 229, 233; Misulia, *Columbus, Georgia*, 117, 160; Williams, *Rich Man's War*, 81. Exactly where Union troopers took possession of the *Viper* is not currently known. Accounts of the Battle of Columbus indicate that several Confederate officers attempted to escape southward, allegedly to Eufaula, on it during the fighting but apparently abandoned the effort and grounded the boat before proceeding too far. Several histories mention that the boat was captured in Eufaula, but there is no documentation confirming this assertion. The boat is not mentioned in Grierson's report on his time in Eufaula or his postwar reminiscences. General Edward Winslow's report of Confederate property seized in Columbus, written on April 18, 1865, only mentions that the boat "went down the river" before the capture of the city on the night of April 16. It does, however, note that the boat was "new and in readiness for active duty." See U.S. War Department, *Official Records*, series I, vol. 49, part 1, 485–87.

122. Hinges and Leckie, *Just and Righteous Cause*, 337–38; Dorman, *History of Barbour County*, 248; Smartt, *History of Eufaula*, 80; Flewellen, *Along Broad Street*, 89; Walker, *Backtracking in Barbour County*, 205.

123. Interviews with former slaves Gus Askew and Hannah Irwin, Federal Writer's Project; Dorman, *History of Barbour County*, 244; Flewellen, *Along Broad Street*, 89.

124. Dorman, *History of Barbour County*, 245; Smartt, *History of Eufaula*, 79–80; U.S. War Department, *Official Records*, series I, vol. 49, part 2, 100; Mollie Young to H.M. Weedon, June 18, 1865, in Weedon Papers, Auburn University Special Collections and Archives.

125. U.S. War Department, *Official Records*, series I, vol. 49, part 1, 372; Walker, *Backtracking in Barbour County*, 209.

126. Hague, *Blockaded Family*, 165; 175; U.S. War Department, *Official Records*, series I, vol. 49, part 1, 302, and part 2, 583–85.

127. Mathis, *John Horry Dent*, 211–12; Davis, "James Lawrence Pugh," 46; U.S. War Department, *Official Records*, series I, vol. 49, part 1, 302; Hague, *Blockaded Family*, 165–66; Walker, *Backtracking in Barbour County*, 222; Clayton, *Black and White Under the Old Regime*, 152.

128. Walmsley, *Experiences of a Civil War Horse-Soldier*, 152; Hague, *Blockaded Family*, 164; Clayton, *Black and White Under the Old Regime*, 152.

129. Smartt, *History of Eufaula*, 74, 81, 88; Walker, *Backtracking in Barbour County*, 203, 212, 218–19; Smith, *Eufaula Album*, 17. Oates's experiences are chronicled in LaFantasie, *Gettysburg Requiem*.

130. Confederados Collection, Auburn University Special Collections and Archives. For more on former Confederate immigration to South America, see Dawsey and Dawsey, *Confederados*.

131. Smartt, *History of Eufaula*, 85; Walker, *Backtracking in Barbour County*, 77, 219–21; Hague, *Blockaded Family*, 166. According to one local source, John G. Archibald was listed on the Confederate Roll of Honor for his meritorious service. I have not been able to confirm this information. For more on Archibald's service record, see Oates, *War Between the Union and the Confederacy*, 711.

Epilogue

132. Eufaula City Council Minutes Record Books, Mayor's Office, City of Eufaula.

133. Hague, *Blockaded Family*, 2; Smartt, *History of Eufaula*, 89.

134. Besson, *History of Eufaula, Alabama*, 20, 25. For information on the formation of the Eufaula Heritage Association and the organization of the Eufaula Pilgrimage, see Smith, *Brief History of Shorter Mansion*.

135. Following is the text of the inscriptions contained on the monument. East face: "This monument is erected by the Barbour County Chapter of the U.D.C. to the Confederate Soldiers of America 1861–1865. Who, true to the promptings of patriotism glorified a fallen cause by the patient endurance of hardship and the willing sacrifice of their lives in the dark hours of imprisonment in the agony of the hospital in the carnage of the field. They found cheering consolation in knowing that at home they would not be forgotten." South face: "Our Naval Heroes. The Southern Confederacy 1861–1865. These were the men whom power could not corrupt whom death could not terrify and whom defeat could not dishonor. They glorified the cause for which they fought. When their voyage of life is o'er may they be welcomed to that shore where the storms are hushed and billows break no more." West face: "To the Unknown Dead. This shaft we consecrated to all who fought. The nameless and the famed in consciousness of right." North face: "This monument perpetuates the memory of those who true to the instinct of their fathers constant in their love for the state died in the performance of their duty."

Bibliography

Books and Articles

Included here is a selection of the primary publications consulted in the compilation of this book. There are dozens of other volumes providing contextual information on events discussed within it that might have been included. One, William Warren Rogers's Confederate Homefront: Montgomery During the Civil War *(Tuscaloosa: University of Alabama Press, 2001), merits mention as it helped provide a model for the structure and scope of this publication.*

Anderson, Lawrence M. *Federalism, Secession and the American State: Divided We Secede.* New York: Routledge, 2013.

Andrews, Eliza Frances. *The War-Time Journal of a Georgia Girl, 1864–1865.* Edited by Spencer Bidwell King Jr. New York: D. Appleton and Company, 1908.

Barney, William L. *The Secessionist Impulse: Alabama and Mississippi in 1860.* Tuscaloosa: University of Alabama Press, 2004.

Barrow, Charles Kelly, J.H. Segars and R.B. Rosenburg. *Black Confederates.* Gretna, LA: Pelican Publishing, 1995.

Beck, Brandon H. *Third Alabama!: The Civil War Memoir of Brigadier General Cullen Andrews Battle, CSA.* Tuscaloosa: University of Alabama Press, 2002.

Besson, J.A.B. *A History of Eufaula, Alabama: The Bluff City on the Chattahoochee.* Atlanta, GA: Harrison and Company, 1875.

Booth, Charles Octavius. *The Cyclopedia of Colored Baptists: Their Leaders and Their Work.* Birmingham: Alabama Publishing Company, 1895.

Brannen, Ralph N. "John Gill Shorter: War Governor of Alabama, 1861–63." Master's thesis, Auburn University, 1956.

Bunn, Mike. *The "Eufaula Regency": Alabama's Most Celebrated Secessionist Faction.* Eufaula, AL: Eufaula Heritage Association, 2009.

Burton, Annie L. *Memories of Childhood Slavery Days.* Whitefish, MT: Kessinger Publishing, 2010.

Campbell, R. Thomas. *Voices of the Confederate Navy: Articles, Letters, Reports, and Reminiscences.* Jefferson, NC: McFarland and Company, 2008.

Carey, Anthony Gene. *Sold Down the River: Slavery in the Lower Chattahoochee of Alabama and Georgia.* Tuscaloosa: University of Alabama Press, 2011.

Claiborne, John Francis Hamtramck. *Life and Correspondence of John A. Quitman.* New York: Harper and Brothers, 1860.

Clayton, Victoria. *White and Black Under the Old Regime.* Milwaukee, WI: Young Churchman Company, 1899.

Crook, Charles M. *Fendall Hall: A True Story of Good Times and Bad Times on the Chattahoochee River.* Montgomery, AL: Charles M. Crook, 2004.

Darden, David L., ed. "The Alabama Secession Convention." *Alabama Historical Quarterly* 3 (Fall and Winter 1941).

Davidson, Mary Jane. "James Lawrence Pugh: A Half Century of Politics." Master's thesis, Auburn University, 1971).

Davis, William C. *A Government of Our Own: The Making of the Confederacy.* New York: Free Press, 1994.

———. *Rhett: The Turbulent Life and Times of a Fire-Eater.* Columbia: University of South Carolina Press, 2001.

Dawsey, Cyrus B., and James M. Dawsey. *The Confederados: Old South Immigrants in Brazil.* Tuscaloosa: University of Alabama Press, 1995.

Denman, Clarence Phillips. *The Secession Movement in Alabama.* Montgomery: Alabama Department of Archives and History, 1933.

Denney, Robert E. *The Distaff Civil War.* Bloomington, IN: Trafford Publishing, 2006.

Detzer, David. *Allegiance: Fort Sumter, Charleston, and the Beginning of the Civil War.* New York: Harcourt, 2002.

Dew, Charles B. *Apostles of Disunion: Southern Secession Commissioners and the Causes of the Civil War.* Charlottesville: University of Virginia Press, 2002.

Dinges, Bruce J., and Shirlie A. Leckie, eds. *A Just and Righteous Cause: Benjamin H. Grierson's Civil War Memoir.* Carbondale: Southern Illinois University, 2008.

Dorman, Lewy. *History of Barbour County, Alabama.* Eufaula, AL: Barbour County Genealogy and Local History Society and Friends of the Library Genealogical Committee, 2006.

———. *Party Politics in Alabama from 1850 through 1860.* Wetumpka, AL: Wetumpka Printing Company, 1935.

DuBose, John Witherspoon. *The Life and Times of William Lowndes Yancey: A History of Political Parties in the United States, from 1834 to 1864; Especially as to the Origin of the Confederate States.* Birmingham, AL: Roberts and Son, 1892.

Eufaula Heritage Association. *The Diaries of Elizabeth Rhodes: Depicting Her Life and Times in the South from 1858 to 1900.* Dothan, AL: Image Agency, 2013.

———. *Historic Eufaula: A Treasury of Southern Architecture, 1827–1910.* Eufaula, AL: self-published, 1972.

Flannery, Michael A. *Civil War Pharmacy: A History of Drugs, Drug Supply and Provision, and Therapeutics for the Union and Confederacy.* Binghamton, NY: Haworth Press, 2004.

Fleming, Walter Lynwood. "The Buford Expedition to Kansas." *American Historical Review* 6, no. 1 (October 1900).

———. *Civil War and Reconstruction in Alabama.* New York: Columbia University Press, 1905.

Flewellen, Robert H. *Along Broad Street: A History of Eufaula, Alabama 1823–1984.* Eufaula, AL: City of Eufaula, 1991.

Frank, Lisa Tendrich, ed. *Women in the American Civil War.* Santa Barbara, CA: ABC-Clio, 2007.

Freehling, William. W. *The Road to Disunion: Secessionist Triumphant, 1854–1861.* New York: Oxford University Press, 2007.

George, Robert Hudson. *Brown University on the Eve of the Civil War: Brunonians in Confederate Ranks, 1861–1865.* Providence, RI: Brown University, 1965.

Hague, Parthenia Antoinette. *A Blockaded Family: Life in Southern Alabama During the Civil War.* Carlisle, MA: Applewood Books, 1995.

Hamilton, Virginia Van der Veer. *Alabama: A History.* New York: W.W. Norton and Company, 1977.

Harden, Edward Jenkins. *The Life of George M. Troup.* Savannah, GA: E.J. Purse, 1859.

Hodgson, Joseph. *Cradle of the Confederacy: The Times of Troup, Quitman and Yancey.* Mobile, AL: Mobile Register, 1876.

Horn, Alan T., John M. Hutcheson, John Phil McLaney Jr. and Robert G. McLendon Jr. *The Yankees Are Coming! The Union Invasion of South Alabama in 1865: A History of General Grierson's March from Ft. Blakeley through Greeneville, Troy, Louisville, Clayton, Eufaula, and Union Springs, Alabama, April 9–May 1, 1865.* Troy, AL: Pike County Historical Society, 2011.

Imboden, John D. "The Treatment of Prisoners During the War Between the States." *Southern Historical Society Papers* 1, no. 3 (March 1876). Southern Historical Society, Richmond, Virginia.

Isham, Asa Brainerd. *Care of Prisoners of War, North and South.* Cincinnati, OH: H.C. Sherick and Company, 1887.

Jennings, Thelma. *The Nashville Convention: Southern Movement for Unity, 1848–1851.* Memphis, TN: Memphis State University, 1980.

Jones, James Pickett. *Yankee Blitzkrieg: Wilson's Raid through Alabama and Georgia.* Lexington: University of Kentucky Press, 1976.

LaFantasie, Glenn W. *Gettysburg Requiem: The Life and Lost Causes of Confederate Colonel William C. Oates.* New York: Oxford University Press, 2006.

Mabelitini, Brian. "The Confederate Fortification of the Apalachicola River, 1861–1865." *Pensacola and Northwest Florida History Illustrated* (Fall 2013): 1–12.

Marvel, William. *Andersonville: The Last Depot.* Chapel Hill: University of North Carolina Press, 1994.

Mathis, Gerald Ray. *In the Land of the Living: Wartime Letters by Confederates from the Chattahoochee Valley of Alabama and Georgia.* Troy, AL: Troy State University Press, 1981.

———. *John Horry Dent: South Carolina Aristocrat on the Alabama Frontier.* Tuscaloosa: University of Alabama Press, 1979.

Mayer, Henry. "A Leaven of Disunion: The Growth of the Secessionist Faction in Alabama, 1847–1851." *Alabama Review* 22 (April 1969).

May, Robert E. *John A. Quitman: Old South Crusader.* Baton Rouge: Louisiana State University Press, 1985.

McCorries, Edward Young. *History of the First Regiment, Alabama Volunteer Infantry, CSA.* Montgomery, AL: Brown Printing, 1904.

McKiven, Henry M., Jr. "John Gill Shorter." Encyclopedia of Alabama. http://www.encyclopediaofalabama.org.

McMillan, Malcolm C. *The Alabama Confederate Reader.* Tuscaloosa: University of Alabama Press, 1963.

————. *Disintegration of a Confederate State: Three Governors of Alabama's Wartime Home Front, 1861–1865.* Macon, GA: Mercer University Press, 1986.

Misulia Charles. *Columbus, Georgia 1865: The Last True Battle of the Civil War.* Tuscaloosa: University of Alabama Press, 2010.

Moore, Albert Burton. *History of Alabama.* Tuscaloosa, AL: University Supply Store, 1934.

Mueller, Ed. *Perilous Journeys: A History of Steamboating on the Chattahoochee, Apalachicola, and Flint Rivers, 1828–1928.* Eufaula, AL: Historic Chattahoochee Commission, 1990.

Napier, John H., III. "Martial Montgomery: Ante Bellum Military Activity." *Alabama Historical Quarterly* 29 (Fall and Winter 1967).

Oates, William C. *The War Between the Union and the Confederacy.* Dayton, OH: Morningside Bookshop, 1974.

Owens, Harry Philpot. "A History of Eufaula, Alabama, 1832–1882." Master's thesis, Auburn University, 1963.

Owen, Thomas M., ed. *Report of the Alabama History Commission to the Governor of Alabama.* Montgomery, AL: Brown Printing Company, 1901.

Perry, Mark. *Conceived in Liberty: Joshua Chamberlain, William Oates, and the American Civil War.* New York: Viking Press, 1997.

Rachleff, Marshall J. "Racial Fear and Political Factionalism: A Study of the Secession Movement in Alabama, 1819–1861." PhD diss., University of Massachusetts, 1974.

Rogers, William Warren, Sr., Leah Rawls Atkins, Robert D. Ward and Wayne Flynt. *Alabama: The History of a Deep South State.* Tuscaloosa: University of Alabama Press, 1994.

Schroeder-Lein, Glenna R. *Confederate Hospitals on the Move: Samuel H. Stout and Army of Tennessee.* Columbia: University of South Carolina Press, 1994.

Smartt, Eugenia Persons. *History of Eufaula, Alabama.* Birmingham, AL: Roberts and Son, 1933.

Smith, Joel P. *A Brief History of Shorter Mansion and the Eufaula Heritage Association.* Eufaula, AL: Eufaula Heritage Association, 2008.

————. *Candid Comments: Selected Articles from* The Eufaula Tribune, *1958–2006.* Montgomery, AL: NewSouth Books, 2011.

————. *A Eufaula Album: A Pictorial History of Eufaula, Alabama.* Eufaula, AL: Eufaula Tribune, 1999.

Smith, William R. *History and Debates of the Convention of People of Alabama.* Montgomery, AL: White, Pfister and Company, 1861.

Speer, Lonnie R. *War of Vengeance: Acts of Retaliation Against Civil War POWs.* Mechanicsburg, PA: Stackpole Books, 2002.

Thompson, Mattie Thomas. *History of Barbour County, Alabama*. Eufaula, AL, 1939.

Thornton, J. Mills, III. *Politics and Power in a Slave Society: Alabama 1800–1860*. Baton Rouge: Louisiana State University Press, 1981.

Tucker, Spencer C. *Brigadier General John D. Imboden: Confederate Commander in the Shenandoah*. Lexington: University of Kentucky Press, 2003.

Turner, Maxine. *Navy Gray: A Story of the Confederate Navy on the Chattahoochee and Apalachicola Rivers*. Tuscaloosa: University of Alabama Press, 1988.

United States Naval War Records Office. *Official Records of the Union and Confederate Navies in the War of the Rebellion*. Series I, volume 17. Washington, D.C.: Government Printing Office, 1903.

United States War Department. *The War of the Rebellion: A Compilation of the Official Records of the Union and Confederate Armies*. Series IV, volume 1, part 1. Washington, D.C.: Government Printing Office, 1901.

Walker, Anne Kendrick. *Backtracking in Barbour County: A Narrative of the Last Alabama Frontier*. Richmond, VA: Dietz Press, 1941.

Walmsley, George Phillip. *Experiences of a Civil War Horse-Soldier*. Lanham, MD: University Press of America, 1993.

Walther, Eric H. *The Fire-Eaters*. Baton Rouge: Louisiana State University Press, 1992.

———. *William L. Yancey and the Coming of the Civil War*. Chapel Hill: University of North Carolina Press, 2006.

Webb, Samuel L., and Margaret E. Armbrester. *Alabama Governors: A Political History of the State*. Tuscaloosa: University of Alabama Press, 2001.

Williams, David. *Rich Man's War: Class, Caste, and Confederate Defeat in the Lower Chattahoochee Valley*. Athens: University of Georgia Press, 1999.

Williams, Horace Randall, ed. *Weren't No Good Times: Personal Accounts of Slavery in Alabama*. Winston-Salem, NC: John F. Blair, 2004.

Yearns, W. Buck, ed. *The Confederate Governors*. Athens: University of Georgia Press, 2010.

Manuscript and Rare Book Collections Consulted

Alabama Department of Archives and History, Montgomery, Alabama.

Columbus Public Library Genealogy and Local History Department, Columbus, Georgia.

Digital Library of Georgia, University of Georgia Libraries, Athens, Georgia.

Eufaula Athenaeum, Eufaula, Alabama.

Eufaula Carnegie Library Genealogy and Local History Room, Eufaula, Alabama.

Library of Congress, Washington, D.C.

Southern Historical Collection at the Wilson Library, University of North Carolina, Chapel Hill, North Carolina.

Special Collections and Archives, Auburn University Libraries, Auburn, Alabama.

W.S. Hoole Special Collections Library, University of Alabama, Tuscaloosa, Alabama.

Index

About the Author

Mike Bunn is the executive director of the Historic Chattahoochee Commission, a state agency of Alabama and Georgia headquartered in Eufaula. He is the author of *The Eufaula Regency: Alabama's Most Celebrated Secessionist Faction* and coauthor of *Battle for the Southern Frontier: The Creek War and the War of 1812* and *Images of America: Lower Chattahoochee River*. He has worked with a wide variety of public and private historical institutions in Alabama, Georgia and Mississippi during his career that have been devoted to interpreting southern history. Mike obtained his undergraduate degree at Faulkner University, earned two master's degrees at the University of Alabama and conducted postgraduate studies at the University of West Georgia. He serves as a board member, representative or volunteer with several cultural heritage organizations on the state, regional and national levels. He lives in Columbus, Georgia, with his wife, Tonya, and daughter, Zoey.